D1441044

Woodcarving
Techniques & Designs

WOODCARVING
TECHNIQUES & DESIGNS

Mike Davies

Hand Books Press
Madison, Wisconsin

Distributed by
North Light Books
Cincinnati, Ohio

First published 1997

ISBN 0-9658248-3-7

02 01 00 99 98 5 4 3 2 1

First published in the U.S. by Hand Books Press
931 E. Main Street #106
Madison, WI 53703–2955

Distributed by North Light Books
An imprint of F&W Publications
1507 Dana Avenue
Cincinnati, OH 45207
TEL 800-289-0963 FAX 513-531-4082

Printed in Hong Kong

Acknowledgements

Now that *Woodcarving By Numbers* is complete, I can take the time to reflect on all the help I have received during the two years I worked on it. I am both proud and grateful that my aim of providing a book to assist woodcarvers at all levels to reach their goals has finally become a reality. But it would not have been possible without the support of family, friends and colleagues, all of whom have contributed in some way.

I would like to thank first of all the gentleman who trained me as a woodcarver, Ron Hester. A true friend, he spent many years equipping me with the skills to carve for myself a wonderful career.

My thanks must also be extended to *Traditional Woodworking* magazine, which has published all the articles I have submitted. I am deeply grateful to Tom Davis of MEC Tools, which manufactures my range of tools to such high standards, and to Christian Driscoll and Ben Macey of Chimera Video Productions who produced and directed the video which complements this book. My thanks go to Tim Gittins and Gary Strawford who provided guidance with the content of both the book and the video.

I am thankful to Abigail Glover, my Commissioning Editor, who has provided tremendous support at every step, making the daunting task of compiling the book both enjoyable and rewarding. Thanks must also go to Ben Jennings for producing the superb photography and to Kerry and Peter Ling of Hothouse Image and Simon Gator Illustrations for their excellent artwork.

Last but by no means least, my final thank you goes to my partner, Sharon, who has tirelessly suffered the months of late nights and weekend work the book demanded. Thank you for checking every single word and for being an incredible source of motivation and a tower of strength.

CONTENTS

Foreword

Woodcarving is one of the earliest and most enduring skills known to man. It is a craft practised by almost every country and culture in the world. From the carved tombs of the Ancient Egyptians to the elaborate ornament of Grinling Gibbons, woodcarving has been used for everyday items, for art, decoration, and religion. It is as popular today as it's ever been.

When *Traditional Woodworking's* longest running series, *Carving by Numbers*, began in May 1994, it was an immediate hit. Our readers, from furniture makers and carpenters to woodturners and restorers, followed Mike Davies' step-by-step instructions and found they could create beautiful and impressive carvings.

The basic premise was this; carving could be taught to people of all skill levels with the use of a simple set of numbered chisels and clear instructions. It was a simple concept; the wood was marked out, each chisel profile was given a number and the carving began.

There was no confusion over which chisel to choose, or which way it should be held, as each project was provided with a sequence of photographs and accompanying text. Mike gave a brief historical background of the piece to be carved and ran a make your own tools section. He even set up a carving hotline for troubled readers.

In this book you will find a range of projects which can all be made following the carving by numbers guidelines. They will make attractive pieces in their own right and, equally, can be used to decorate wooden furniture and panels or to transform boxes and turned work. Most importantly they are designed for anyone who wants to learn this ancient and graceful skill.

Happy carving!

Helen Adkins
Traditional Woodworking

Introduction

I have often found that people are hesitant about learning to carve partly as a result of the misconception that the craft requires extreme artistic talent. In fact this is not the case – the only thing required is a logical approach.

I am a firm believer in the saying, 'The only way to understand is to do'. This book is therefore designed to provide a course in the basics of the craft through a series of projects which will gradually allow you to build up your skills as well as a collection of varied carvings. Introductory chapters covering tools and techniques provide you with all the information you need to be able to tackle the projects. You can refer to them as often or as little as you wish depending on your level of skill and confidence.

I have selected decorations that are not only excellent learning pieces but also attractive ornamentations with many applications. Moulding projects, for instance, are useful forms of decoration both for the cabinetmaker and for the woodturner. Many of the projects are equally as attractive on their own merits as they would be incorporated into furniture.

I recommend working through the projects in the order in which they appear. They progressively introduce new skills so that by the time you have completed the last in the series you will be well on the way to becoming an accomplished carver.

EQUIPMENT AND TECHNIQUES

Chisels

The extensive range of carving chisels available can make the task of selecting a suitable collection for the beginner daunting. To simplify matters, I have chosen five chisels, each with a straight shaft, as a good foundation set. All the projects in this book can be carved using these numbered chisels. As and when a particular chisel is required, the number reference will be given in the text. You may find it useful to label your own chisel handles clearly with the appropriate numbers for easy reference. Most manufacturers produce carving chisels to the same specifications. The type of chisel is determined by a combination of three factors: the width of the blade; the shape of the blade in cross-section; and the shape of the blade along its shaft. There is a standard numerical referencing system, known as the Sheffield List, which describes each one in terms of the blade in cross-section and the shape of its shaft. The width of the blade is given separately in both imperial and metric. When you buy good quality tools, you should find these details stamped on the metal shaft or, sometimes, at the base of the handle.

Gouges and parting tools (also known as V tools), for example, are available in a range of sizes but, obviously, while the former can also vary in circumference, the latter vary in angle. The Sheffield List is used throughout the UK and, with slight variations, abroad. It is therefore a simple matter to match your own chisels to the profiles shown next to the corresponding chisel in the photograph on this page. Or you can send away for the Carving by Numbers set available from the address on page 143. Of course, as your skills improve and you attempt increasingly challenging projects, you may wish to start adding to your collection.

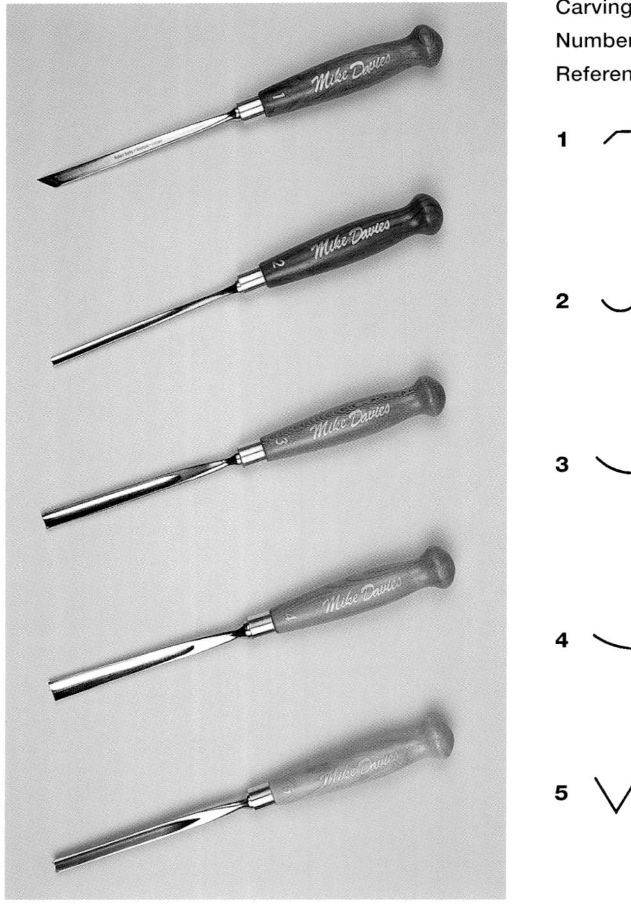

Carving by Numbers Reference

1

2

3

4

5

Sheffield List Reference (From top to bottom)

9mm/$\frac{3}{8}$in (No. 2)
4.5mm/$\frac{3}{16}$in (No. 6)
9mm/$\frac{3}{8}$in (No. 6)
12mm/$\frac{1}{2}$in (No. 5)
6mm/$\frac{1}{4}$in (No. 39)

(Opposite) These are the most commonly used chisel profiles although the Sheffield List is actually even more extensive than it appears here.

Straight Tools	Long Bent Tools	Spoon Bent Tools	Bent Tools
1	–	21	–
2	–		
3	12	24	33
4	13	25	34
5	14	26	35
6	15	27	36
7	16	28	37
8	17	29	38
9	18	30	–
10	19	31	–
11	20	32	–
39	40	43	–
41	42	44	–
45	46	–	–

PROFILES

1/16	1/8	3/16	1/4	5/16	3/8	7/16	1/2	5/8	3/4	1in
1.5	3	4.5	6	8	9	11	12	16	19	25mm

Basic Techniques and Timber Selection

CHISEL TECHNIQUES

I always aim to encourage beginners to learn six basic carving techniques very thoroughly. Practising these teaches people how to hold and use their chisels effectively, safely and, most importantly, in a controlled manner. Once perfected, they will also provide the foundation for developing more advanced skills. They are all used repeatedly throughout the projects.

At first, you may find some of these methods awkward but with a little perseverence you will soon find yourself using them without thinking.

THE PINCH POSITION

The first technique is a way of holding the chisel so as to maximise the efficiency of the cutting edge. Don't worry if you are left or right handed. Just hold the chisel in whichever hand feels most comfortable. Pinch the shaft between your fingertips and thumb to provide a firm grip. Your other hand should be used to hold the handle and to apply the controlled pressure needed to make the chisel cut. This technique is used for 'setting in', which basically means that the chisel makes an incision at 90° to the surface of the timber. Setting in should be done very gently at first, lightly marking a pattern on to the wood. You can then apply steadily greater pressure to cut more deeply. The pinch position should also be used for gripping the chisel when removing small amounts of wood. This makes it particularly suitable for fine work.

The pinch position is used mainly for fine work.

Use the pinch position also when you need to set in a fine cut.

THE FIST POSITION

Close your hand around the chisel to make a fist, leaving approximately 25–35mm (1–1 ⅜in) of the chisel shaft from the cutting edge exposed. Remember the cutting edge should always be next to your little finger. This method of holding the chisel provides extra grip when removing large amounts of timber.

The fist position provides extra grip when increased force is required to remove large amounts of timber.

ANCHORING

Apply this technique at all times combined with both the pinch and fist positions. The hand (or forearm of the hand) holding the chisel must always be in contact with the workbench or the timber that is being carved. This provides the chisel with a breaking system or anchor. Notice the hand is pivoted at the wrist when using the fist position.

SLIDING

The sliding technique is used to maximize the efficiency of the chisel's cutting edge. Try cutting a loaf of bread using downward pressure alone. The result would be very ragged and torn. If you use a sliding motion, the cut becomes much more effective. Similarly as you move the chisel forward through the timber, turn the handle from side to side to create a sliding action along the length of the cutting edge. Practise this action initially without cutting into the timber and then apply it to very shallow cuts. The technique proves its worth particularly when carving across the grain.

Slide the chisel in a similar action to cutting a piece of bread with a knife, rotating the wrist from side to side as you work.

Practise by carving a piece of wide and straight grained timber, preferably a softwood such as pine, aiming for a clean cut without signs of tearing. The blade should leave a polished sheen on the surface of the wood.

Practise using both hands to carve. Hold the chisel in the left hand to work towards your left.

Hold the chisel in the right hand to work towards your right.

BECOMING AMBIDEXTROUS

The final technique is potentially the most awkward and will probably require more practice than the others. However, if you are to work efficiently you will certainly need to be able to use both hands with equal confidence.

The photographs show how to work with both hands when carving a barley twist, but the same method should be applied to any project whether it happens to be as small as the basic flower shown on pages 46–7 or larger and more complex like the decorative bracket shown on pages 100–103. In this instance the fist position is being used and the chisel is gripped with the left hand to carve to the left-hand side of the bench and vice versa for the right. Mastering the technique of using both hands without having to think about it enables you to remain centrally located in front of your work and avoids the need for you to lean over the bench or to reposition the carving at regular intervals.

TAPPING

When moving the chisel forward, never apply a greater force than your controlled arm weight. It is dangerous to use your body weight since your anchor will be unable to withstand such force. If greater pressure is required, a mallet should be used.

The tapping technique combines the fist and anchoring positions. Grip the chisel in the fist position, making sure your forearm is correctly anchored, and gently tap the handle of the chisel with a mallet. The chisel will be pushed forward by the tap, making a cut, but the anchor will immediately force it to return to its original position. This provides a controlled burst of power and when the cut needs to be advanced, the anchor can be relocated.

The tapping technique is used to drive the chisel through the wood when greater pressure is required than the weight of your arm.

CUTTING DIRECTIONS

It will not take you very long to realise that most timbers tend to work rather better in one direction than the other. Timber such as oak for example, may plane beautifully one way leaving a a smooth surface and a polished sheen from the blade. However, if you try to plane in the opposite direction, the grain may lift, producing sporadic tears and pitted areas. The same problem will also occur when carving a piece of wood with a chisel, making the process frustrating as well as leaving you with a difficult task in terms of repairing the damaged surface of the wood. Although it is only common sense to try always to carve in the best direction, on certain projects, such as mouldings (see pages 48 and 50), it is often impossible. This is where the sliding technique illustrated on page 13 comes into play.

To overcome this problem you must first understand how the timber is formed. This, in turn, will help you to make decisions about the appropriate direction to cut.

Figs. 1–3 A cut is always more effective when it is directed from short grain to long.

Imagine a piece of wood as being a bundle of long drinking straws, the length of the straws representing the direction of the grain. Figs. 1–3 show that the cut will always be more effective when it is directed from short grain (straws) to long. As you can see in Fig. 2, working in the correct direction produces a smooth, clean cut while working from long grain to short as shown in Fig. 3 will result in a ragged cut.

Fig. 2

Fig. 3

FIRST CUTS

Before you tackle the various projects it is good practice to familiarize yourself with the chisels and the six basic techniques. The following exercise is also ideal to test the sharpness of the chisels.

- Secure a piece of timber to the work surface and, with whichever hand you feel most comfortable, hold chisel No. 3 in the fist position. Slide the chisel through the timber in the direction of the grain, making sure that you anchor. Remove small scoops at a time, moving the chisel with controlled arm weight only. If you find that you need to apply body weight, you are trying to remove too much timber in one go.

- Next carve across the grain using the sliding technique, attempting to remove timber from different directions. If you need to carve further than your anchor hand will allow, relocate it rather than raising it to finish the cut. This will ensure a 'breaking system' is in place at all times.

- Now apply the tapping technique in a number of directions. Try to produce clean scoops, formed by a number of taps, without any visible chatter marks from the blade.

- Using the same hand to grip chisel No. 3, change to the pinch position and set in a cut with the chisel shaft at 90°. Remember to use controlled arm weight only with the motivating hand, while anchoring the chisel with the other. Now revert to the fist position and slide the chisel towards the convex side of the first cut. The aim is to remove a clean segment of timber with only two cuts. However, if more cuts are required or if small fragments of timber are left behind, you need to practise the technique.

- Repeat each stage again, but this time hold the chisel in the opposite hand. With perseverance the techniques will gradually become easier.

Test your chisels on a block of wood, practising making cuts in all directions both across and with the grain.

TIMBER SELECTION

There are, without doubt, better woods to carve than others. Lime, basswood, Honduras mahogany, North American tulipwood and certain pines are all commonly favoured by carvers. Timbers that are light in weight with close, straight grain configurations are generally ideal for beginners, but may not look as interesting as others when polished. Dense timbers with interesting grain configurations on the other hand tend to be more awkward.
Do not be fooled by the terms 'softwood' and 'hardwood'. A softwood actually means that the tree is coniferous, retaining its foliage throughout the year. Hardwoods on the other hand are deciduous trees, which lose their leaves during the winter months. This categorization is no indication of the density of the timber, which is illustrated by the fact that balsa is a hardwood.

The best way to determine a good carving wood is actually to take a few scoops with a sharp gouge out of various samples. This may not always be possible before you purchase, however, unless you are on particularly good terms with your local supplier. If you are able to test a few pieces of wood before buying or if you have an alternative source of supply, such as wood from a storm-felled tree in your own or a neighbour's garden, try carving in all directions, particularly across the grain, to determine which pieces are the best. Try not to condemn an entire species simply because the sample you have chosen happens to be awkward. It may have been stored badly in very dry conditions and become brittle. Lime, for instance, is known for being like butter to carve but if stored in very dry conditions it may become crumbly. If your timber choice is a good one, the grain should not bruise, pit or tear.

Another consideration when selecting a suitable timber is the location of the finished carving. This is particularly important when the carving is to be used on furniture that is functional or positioned in places where it is vulnerable to damage. A softer wood, for instance, may be incapable of withstanding continual knocks and the pressure of admiring hands.

Sharpening and Tool Maintenance

Carving wood with blunt tools can be compared to slicing a loaf of bread with a spoon. The key to all good carving and the proficiency of any carver is dependent on the sharpness of the chisels. The cutting edges should do the work – in a sense, you are merely there to support and guide them.

You will need to be able to identify the faults in a cutting edge. The illustration below shows a blade with a number of serious defects.

There are many products on the market which are effective in producing a razor finish. However, a basic knowledge of sharpening is essential for all. The following information identifies the series of stages which should be used as appropriate.

1 **The ground angle of the cutting edge is too great. The ideal angle varies between 20 and 30°. The flexibility of 10° is subject to the hardness of the timber to be carved. Obviously the smaller the angle, the weaker the edge becomes. A general guideline is that the length of the bevel should be around twice the thickness of the chisel's blade.**

2 **It is generally desirable for the cutting edge to form a 90° angle to the chisel's shaft with the exception of a skew chisel (page 10).**

3 **The blade has been chipped possibly by carving a piece of grit embedded in the timber, or it may mean that the chisel's angle is too small for the density of the timber. In the worst scenario the metal may have become brittle, so if the blade continues to chip, it will need re-tempering. A perfectly clean straight cutting edge should be attained.**

4 **The outside tips of the cutting edge have become rounded over. They should be square and intact, forming pointed corners.**

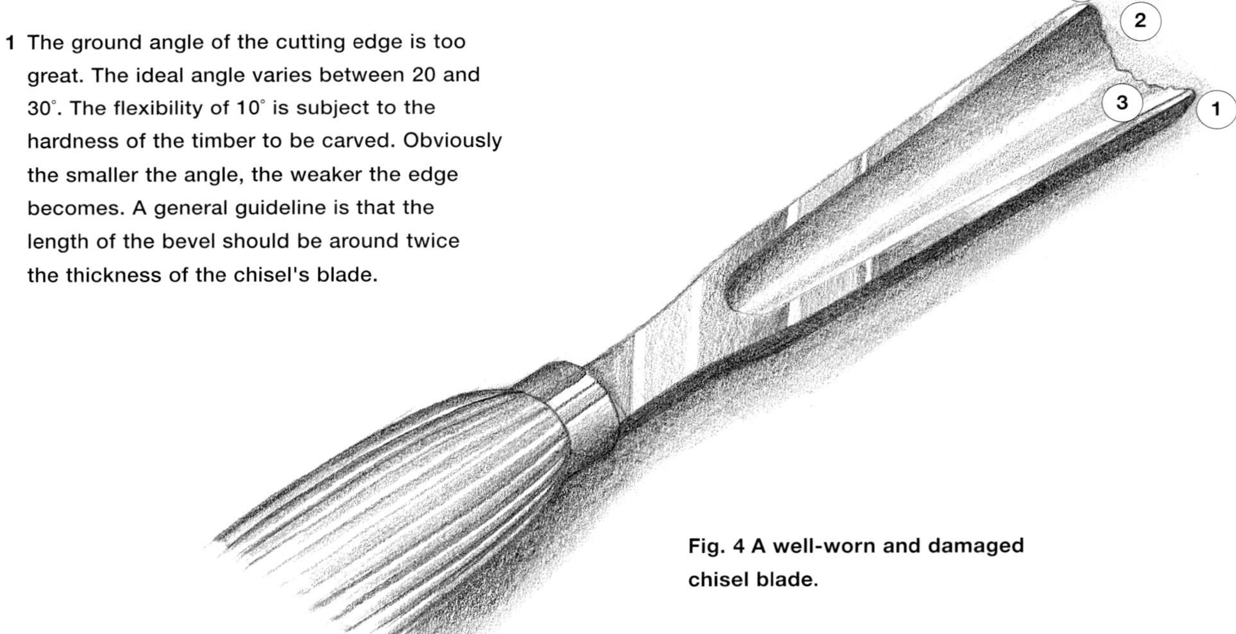

Fig. 4 A well-worn and damaged chisel blade.

GRINDING

There are two main categories of grinding machines; dry grinders and wet-wheeled grinding machines. Both are extremely effective for removing metal quickly. However, if used incorrectly, the dry-wheeled grinder will heat the metal blade with potentially disastrous effects.

The steel of a chisel is manufactured in such a way that it is strong without being brittle. This process is known as tempering. When the blade is reheated, it will lose this quality and become susceptible to chipping. It is, therefore, essential when grinding with a dry wheel to constantly dip the blade into a container of water to cool the edge. A wet-wheeled grinder is fitted with a trough of water, providing a constant flow of liquid to the blade, ensuring it is kept cool.

Always follow the machine manufacturer's guidelines, which include:

- wearing safety goggles and ear protection
- ensuring all loose clothing is tucked away
- keeping clear of moving components

1 Whilst the machine is switched off, pivot the blade on the tool rest so that the end touches the grinding wheel.

2 Establish the appropriate angle and hold the chisel shaft firmly between your forefinger and thumb. Pinch the blade so the forefinger is against the tool rest. Hold this position until the grind has been completed, even when removing the chisel from the machine to cool the blade. Your forefinger provides a stop against the machine rest, ensuring a continuous grinding angle.

3 Turn the machine on and commence grinding. If grinding a gouge, rotate the hand supporting the handle for even treatment around the entire cutting edge.

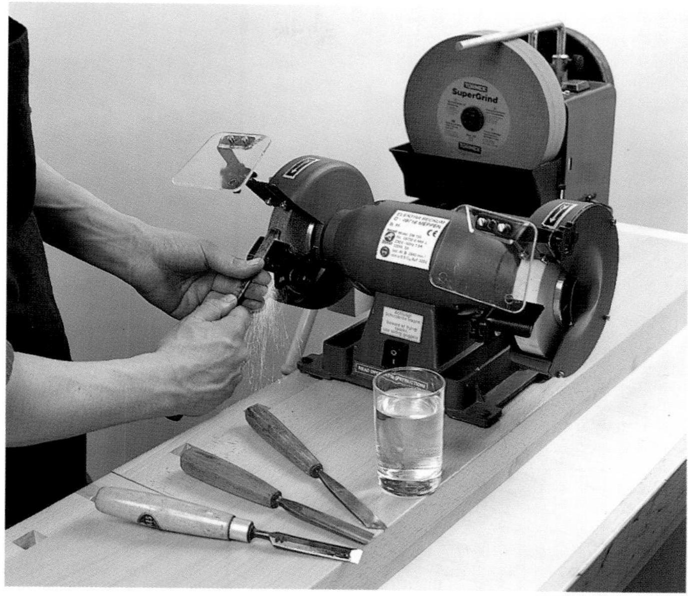

Rotate the wrist gently if grinding a curved chisel blade. Note how the forefinger of the hand holding the chisel acts as a stop against the tool rest. Have a container of water at hand to cool the metal. (Behind the dry grinder being used, you can also see a wet-wheeled grinder.)

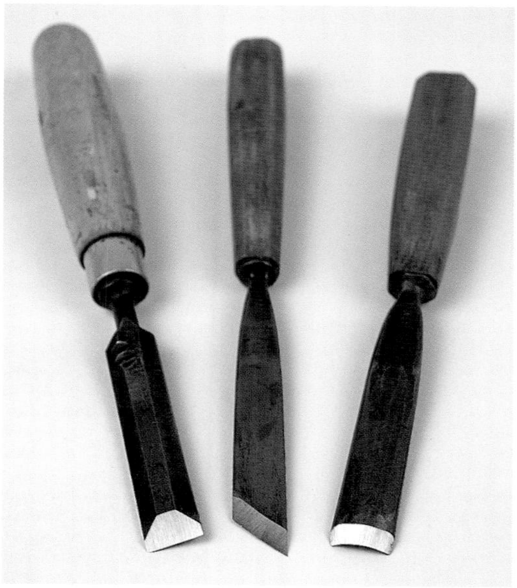

Three correctly ground chisels. Note how the metal of each newly ground bevel shines, displaying an even, consistent angle.

HONING

This process removes less metal and creates a finer edge. In general the honing angle should be the same as the ground angle. To maintain a continuous angle when honing, lock your elbows into your sides and adjust your height with your knees.

Whether you decide to use man made or natural stones, the method of honing will require the same techniques. Most stones require oil or water to be applied to their surface. They act not as lubricants, but to carry away particles of metal and grit.

HONING FLAT CUTTING EDGES

1 Position the stone on your workbench with its length running away from you. Add a little oil or water to the surface according to the manufacturer's instructions.

2 Place the chisel on to the stone's surface at the required angle, and push it back and forth in a continuous motion. It is essential that the same angle is maintained throughout this process. Continue until you are able to feel a small ridge of metal or wire, which will form on the opposite side of the ground angle. This is called a 'burr' and needs to be removed using a slip stone.

HONING CURVED CUTTING EDGES

1 When honing a gouge, fluter or veiner, place the stone horizontally in front of you and add a little oil or water as appropriate.

2 Place the gouge at the required angle on the surface and slide it from side to side along the stone's length. As you slide, rotate the gouge so that the curvature of the blade receives an even grind. Be careful not to hone away the corners of the cutting edge which need to be kept at a sharp 90° angle to the shaft. If the corners become rounded then it is probable that the gouge is being rotated too much. It may be helpful to practise the sliding motion initially on a flat piece of soft wood. When using the stone, continue the process until you can feel the burr on the inside of the gouge's curve, opposite the honed angle. This should be removed with a slipstone.

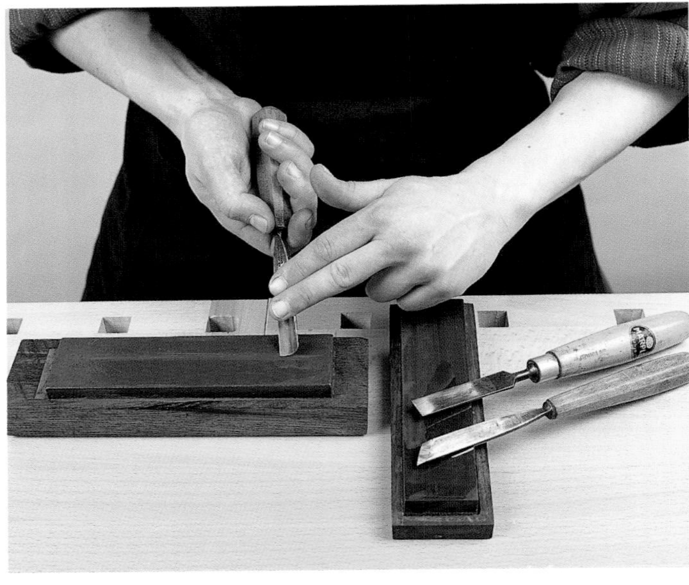

When honing a chisel on an oilstone, slide the chisel back and forth, rotating the wrist to ensure the blade receives even treatment. For flat cutting edges the stone should run lengthwise away from you. For curved cutting edges the stone should run horizontally in front of you.

USING A SLIPSTONE

Slipstones are used to remove burrs and provide a finer cutting edge. The set of five chisels requires only two shapes of slipstone; both should be of a finer grade than that of the benchstone and they must obviously fit inside the chisel profiles.

1 Hold the slipstone between your fingertips and thumb and rub the length of the stone along the inner shaft to remove the burr. It is quite acceptable to form an inner angle on the inside of the gouges. However, I prefer to keep this to a minimum. The main purpose is to remove the burr formed by honing.

2 Rub the slipstone up and down along the ground angle of the chisel, maintaining the same angle to avoid rounding over the cutting edge. Repeat this process until you feel confident that the edge is razor sharp.

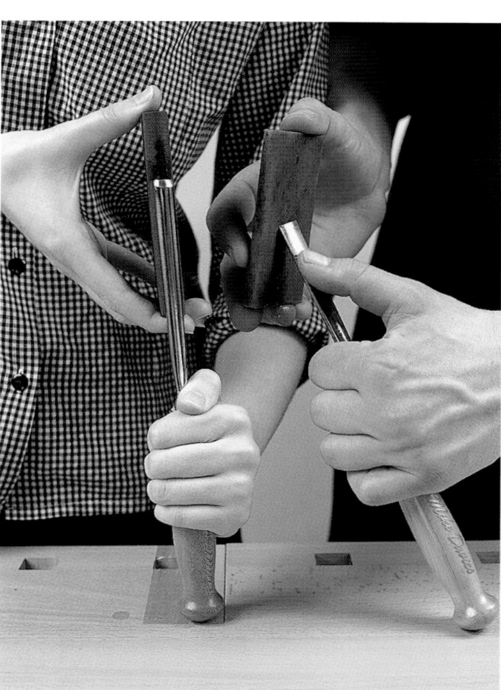

Honing a chisel with shaped slipstones. Left: first hone the inside cutting edge. Right: the next stage is to hone the outside cutting edge.

STROPPING

Stropping removes any remaining traces of burr and adds a final razor finish. Strop the cutting edge by running it several times down a thick piece of leather which has been treated with fine abrasive paste such as Jeweller's Rouge or Crocus powder. For stropping the outside angle, the leather should be placed flat on the bench top, and for inside the blade, wrapped around a compatibly shaped item. A slipstone is useful for this purpose.

The only way to test the sharpness of the chisel is to carve with it. A sharp chisel should produce a polished cut when carving the grain in all directions, whereas a dull tool will leave drag lines. Use the techniques described on page 16 to assess the quality of the cutting edge. If drag lines are evident, then the honing process should be repeated until a razor sharp edge is obtained.

Using a leather strop impregnated with crocus powder to hone the outside cutting edge (left) and the inside cutting edge (right) of a chisel.

SHARPENING EQUIPMENT

A wide range of sharpening equipment is available and a collection of some of the most useful tools and accessories is pictured below and on the opposite page. Select what you need according to your requirements and your budget. Sharpening stones fall into two main categories – natural and man made. Both types are available as benchstones and slipstones, and come in a variety of different grades. A medium grade is ideal for the benchstone whereas a finer grade is more suitable for the slipstone. Man made ceramic stones are just as fine as natural Arkansas stones which can be used to produce a very keen final cutting edge. All stones require the same techniques as described on pages 20–21 though the recommended carrier may vary from oil to water. Follow the instructions supplied by the manufacturer in each case.

Some machines such as the Tormec wet-wheeled grinding machine (see below) are

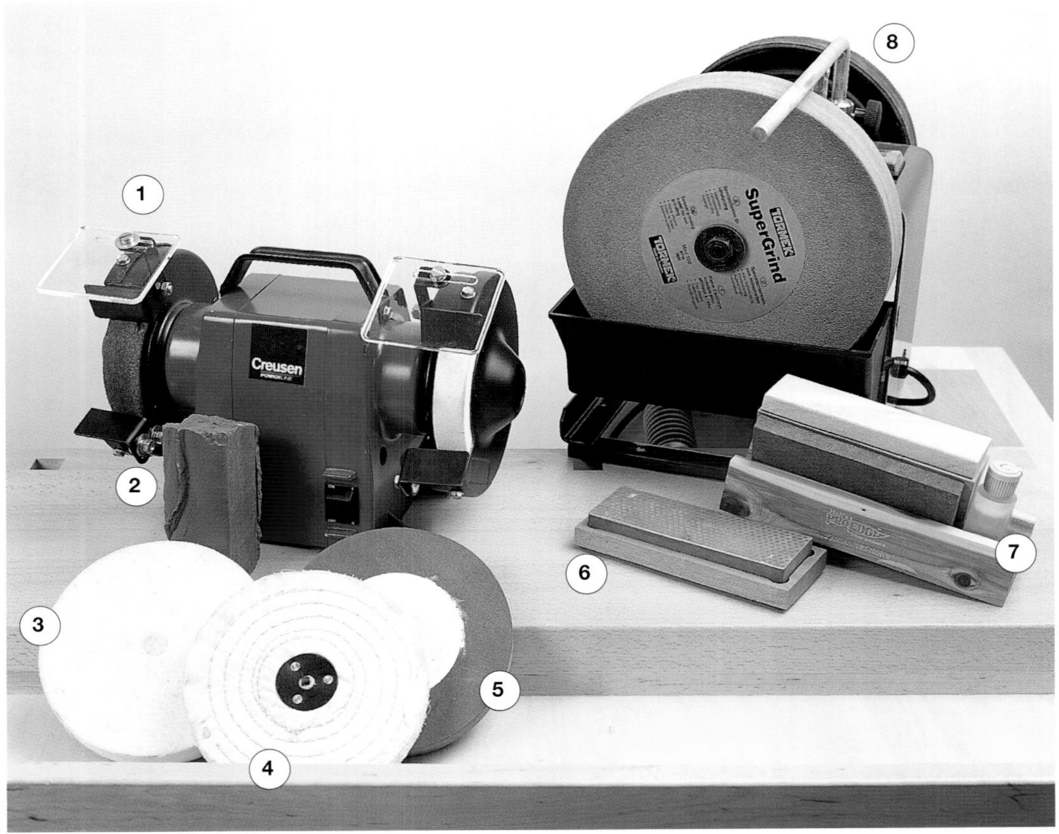

1 Creusen-Koch honing machine
2 Abrasive soap
3 Felt wheel
4 Stitched cloth dolly
5 Rubberised abrasive wheel
6 Diamond sharpening system
7 Arkansas stones
8 Tormec wet-wheeled grinding machine

fitted with a water trough which means that as the wheel turns it carries water to the blade to prevent the metal from overheating. Those without this facility, such as the Record dry bench grinding machine (shown on this page), require the blade being ground to be dipped in water to keep it cool.

The Creusen-Koch honing machine looks exactly the same as a dry grinding machine, but it has a very important difference. The direction in which the wheel turns is away from rather than towards the cutting edge. This means that softer wheels, of fibrous material such as felt, can be fitted to the machine to produce a much finer cut. The material wheels should be impregnated with abrasive soap which is similar to strop compound. It is possible, therefore, to achieve a razor finish straight from the machine using the techniques described in grinding.

1 Record dry bench grinding machine
2 Silicon carbide stones
3 Japanese water stones
4 Ceramic stones
5 Crocus powder
6 Leather strop

Making your own Tools

At one time or another you may come across a problem which could easily be solved if only you had the correct tools. It is often the case, however, that the tool you require is not on the market. Therefore, it is extremely rewarding to make and use the most appropriate tool for the job more cheaply than you could buy it. The tools shown throughout this section will be required in the various projects.

DIVIDERS

You will need:

- two pieces of timber measuring 170 x 30 x 12mm (6 ¾ x 1 ¼ x ½in)
- two nuts and bolts, preferably brass, measuring approximately 20mm (¾in) long with a bolt diameter of 6mm (¼in)
- one nut and bolt, preferably brass, measuring approximately 12mm (½in) long with a bolt diameter of 3mm (⅛in)
- two brass carpet nails measuring 30mm (1 ¼in) in length
- an old secretaire stay from a bureau or 2mm (1/16in) brass sheet to form the arc, as seen in Fig. 11 on page 106

One of the most frequently used tools for carving is a pair of dividers. Whether for marking out purposes or for gauging distances, the dividers are often a treasured part of the woodcarver's tool kit. The following instructions provide you with a unique and relatively simple pair to make. All the components were found scattered around my workshop. The dividers pictured here are made from rose wood, although the choice of wood is entirely your own.

1 Select the timber and prepare it to a thickness of 12mm (½in). Photocopy or redraw Fig. 11 to scale and transfer the outline from the paper to the timber using carbon paper. Ensure the grain runs lengthways on both legs.

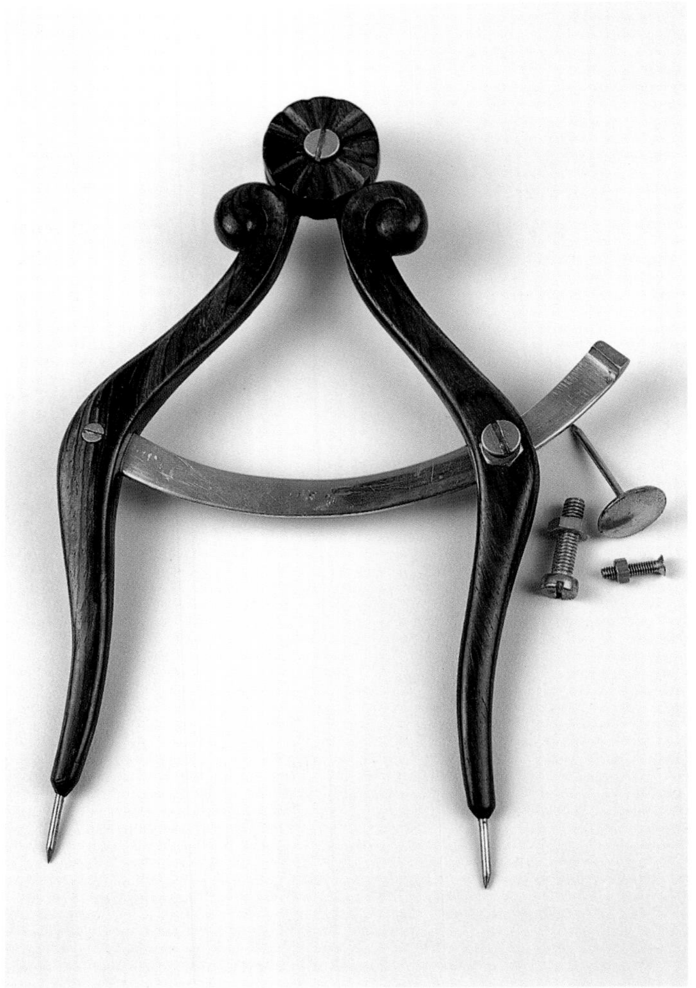

A pair of home-made dividers.

2 Cut the legs out using a coping or band saw and form the joint, as illustrated in Fig. 11. The legs can then be assembled. Drill a hole through the centre of the joint which will enable the brass bolt to be fitted and secured.

3 Using the drawing as reference, mark out and fit the brass arc, securing it through one leg with a small nut and bolt. To provide the locking device, set a nut into the opposite leg ensuring it is an extremely snug fit. This should be secured with a strong adhesive.

4 Fitting the points may be somewhat awkward as it is difficult to align them at the same angle with both ends meeting point to point. To make this process a little easier mark the correct angle on the wood. If you do not have a drill as small as the points, then it is possible to use the points themselves as the drill bit (see page 29). If the points do not meet after fitting, gently bend them into place, being sure to support the surrounding timber to prevent splitting.

5 When you have fitted the brass and it is holding the components together, you can begin to shape the wood. The only carving tools required are those in the carving by numbers set. Use chisel Nos. 2 and 3 to form the scrolls. Shape the legs with chisel Nos. 1 and 4. Form the fan design with chisel No. 1. Finish off with a final sanding and a few coats of polish followed by wax.

SLIPSTONES

You will need:

- small pieces of dense timber. The slipstones illustrated on page 26 were made from 80 x 45 x 10mm (3 ⅛ x 1 ¾ x ⅜in) beech
- fine wet and dry paper

1 Select a small piece of hardwood and shape it to fit inside the profile of the chisel to be sharpened. Both edges of the wood may be used for different profiles.

2 Wrap wet and dry or fine Emery paper around the wooden profile which can be used to remove the burr formed by honing. Although the paper may frequently tear, if held tightly around the wood, it will most definitely serve its purpose.

PUNCHES

You will need:

- various lengths of shaped metal bar. Old brace bits and nails are ideal

Shaped Punches

There are times when you are unable to remove splinters of wood from tiny crevices with a chisel. A simple way of overcoming this problem is to make a punch which fits into the space. When struck with a hammer, the splinters of timber will be compressed to form a clean area. Simply gather a collection of nails or metal bar and file the required shapes into the ends.

Texturing Punches

When observing relief panel carvings you may notice that some have been given a textured background formed by many hundreds of tiny indentations. This textured surface can look effective for two main reasons. Firstly, it gives the carving greater definition and can be made to contrast further if it is stained or polished with coloured wax. The indentations retain the finish more than the carving itself, giving the background a darker colour. Secondly, when carving away the background to bring the panel into relief, it is difficult to clear the waste from some of the smaller recesses and even more difficult to achieve a completely flat background. The texturing, therefore, hides a multitude of sins.

The indentations are formed by metal punches like those shown in the photograph below. These can be made in a variety of different shapes and sizes to fit into any number of awkward places. Old brace bits or large nails can easily be converted into useful punches. You can see that the ends have been filed into grids of small pyramid shapes. This can be done using a triangular saw file. When struck by a hammer into the timber, the punch forms the desired texturing. Here they have been stamped into a piece of scrap wood which has then been stained to enhance the pattern.

PALLET KNIFE

Although the pallet knife is more commonly found in the kitchen cutlery drawer than in a woodcarver's tool kit, it is an extremely useful implement for lifting carvings that have been fixed to the work surface using wax and glue (see page 32). The broad thin blade of the knife makes it ideal for sliding gently underneath the carving to separate the glue joint. Never be tempted to use other thin metal objects for this purpose as they may be more brittle. A hacksaw blade for example could shatter and cause you an injury.

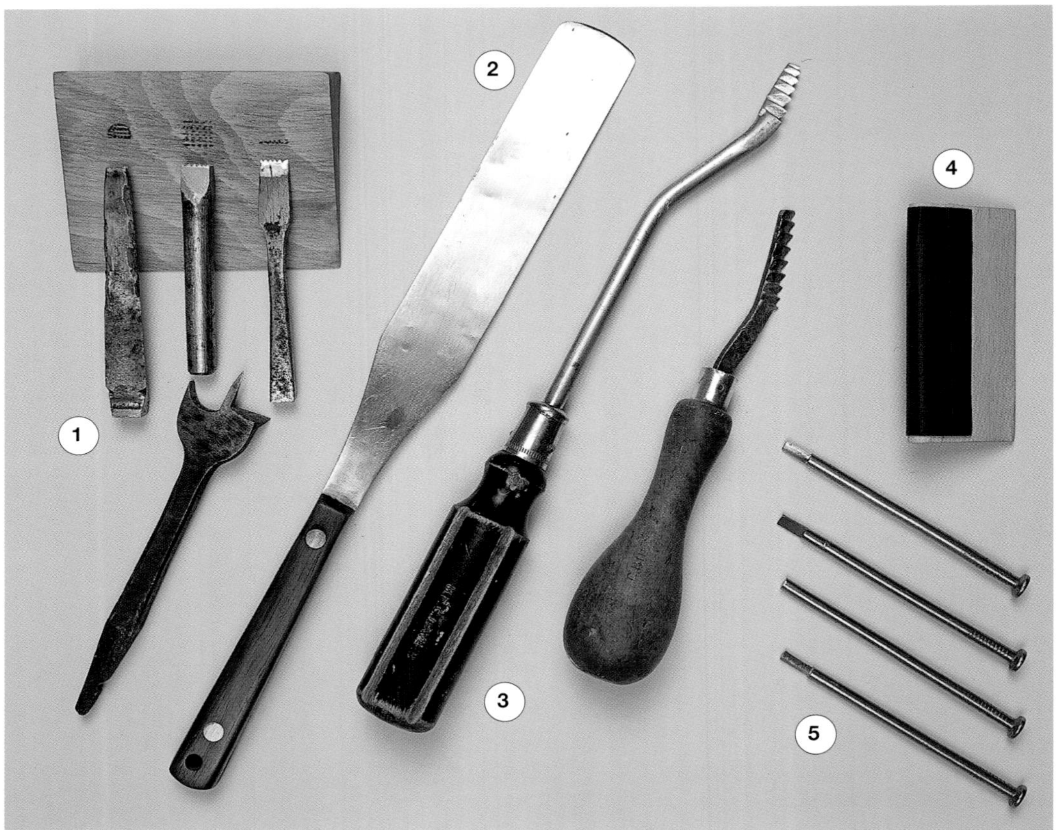

1 Texturing punches
2 Pallet knife
3 Valley tools
4 Slipstones
5 Shaped punches

VALLEY TOOLS

You will need:

- an old screwdriver with a blade measuring approximately 25mm (1in) to cut the teeth into

On projects that require long, perfectly straight grooves, it is difficult to achieve such accuracy using chisel No. 5 alone. Here is a simple-to-make tool which is extremely useful for tidying up 'valleys'.

1. Bend an old screwdriver in the vice to resemble the shape in the picture. You should aim for the edge, where the teeth have been cut, to be parallel with the handle.

2. Hold the screwdriver in the vice and with a triangular shaped saw file, cut a series of grooves on both sides of the screwdriver's blade to form teeth that are similar to a saw. Make sure the grooves are in exactly the same position on both sides. The resulting teeth should be sharp and pointed, running in a perfectly straight line. They should range from fine near the tip of the blade to larger teeth towards the back. When using the tool as a mini saw, you will notice that by running it back and forth it will cut a valley relatively quickly. With all teeth cutting at the same time, the tool helps to keep the valley straight.

STENCILS

You will need:

- thin cardboard, mounting board, or thick paper

To carve a repetative design, it is often difficult and time consuming to mark out every single component by hand. Stencils are simple to make and only require your perseverance with one drawing. Holes can be made on the stencil to provide starting points for internal decoration and they can also be stored for future use.

Simply draw the design on to thin cardboard, and cut it out using scissors. As many of the stencils feature curves which correspond to the exact shapes of the chisel profiles, you can also use your chisels to maintain accuracy when cutting out the cardboard templates.

SPRING CRAMPS

You will need:

- upholsterers spring coils – the larger the better

Occasionally you will need to glue two components together which, due to their awkward shape and size, render a G or sash cramp impracticable. A simple solution lies in an upholsterer's coil spring, which can provide a surprisingly powerful cramp.

Cut the spring into lengths and sharpen both ends to a point using the grinding wheel. You can then reshape the various lengths into C-shaped curves. As you widen the arc of the C it will of course try to revert to its original size, thus applying pressure to the object held in between.

BENCH SCREW

You will need:

- a length of dowel, approximately 20mm (¾in) in diameter and 300mm (12in) in length
- a dowel screw, which is a double pointed screw with a left- and right-handed thread that meets in the middle. The size of the screw will depend on the job you wish to cramp. However, in this case it has an 8mm (5⁄16in) diameter
- a hardwood block measuring approximately 70 x 70 x 50mm (2 ¾ x 2 ¾ x 2in).

Bench screws are available from most of the larger woodworking tool stockists. However, the following will produce a useful home-made alternative.

1 Drill a 'pilot hole' into the end of the dowel and screw in the dowel screw halfway, leaving the opposite handed thread exposed.

2 Using a brace and bit, bore a hole through the centre of the block on its 70mm (2 ¾in) face. The diameter of the hole should be the exact size of the dowel.

3 Mark and cut the block in half with a tenon saw, dividing the hole down the middle. You should find that around 1–2mm (1⁄32–1⁄16in) of wood will be removed, depending on the set of the saw teeth.

When placing the two blocks on either side of the dowel, a small gap is left. This means that a G cramp can be tightened on to the blocks, locking the dowel in a fixed position. To use the home made bench screw, drill a hole through the work surface and insert the dowel from the underside. Then adjust the block so

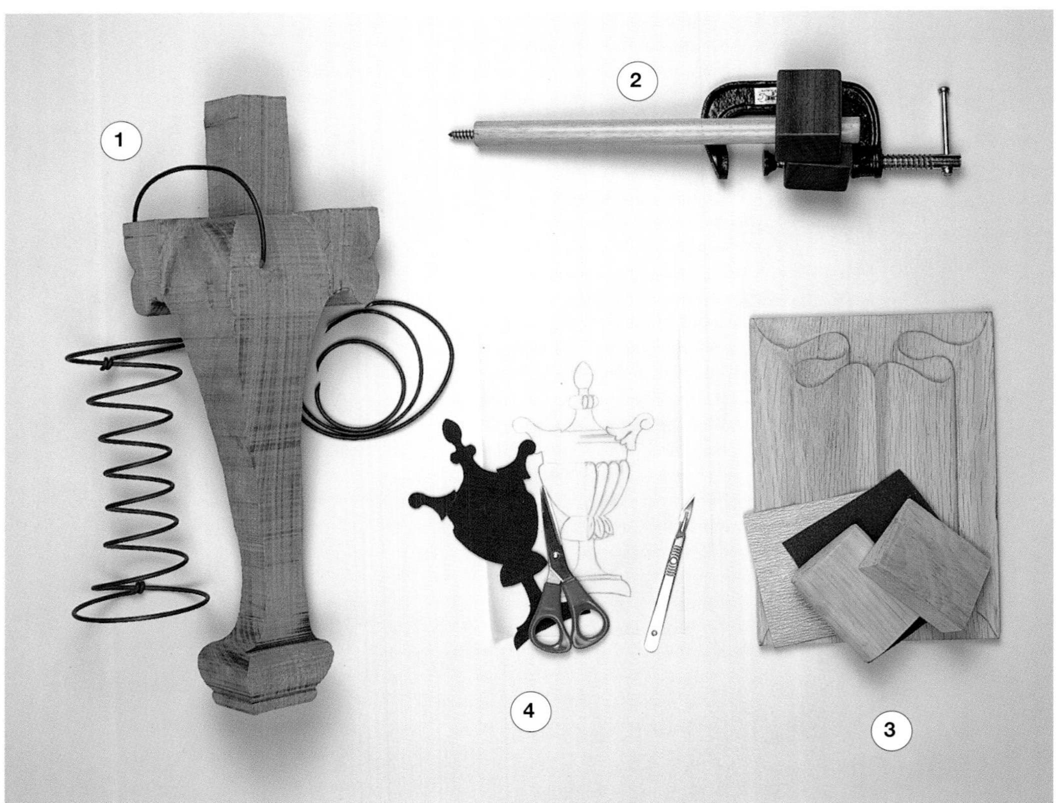

1 Spring cramps
2 Bench screw
3 Sanding blocks
4 Stencil

that only the screw is protruding above. After having made a pilot hole in the base of the carving blank, screw the work on top of the device until it tightens itself to the work surface. When drilling a hole into the bench, it is important to ensure that you do not bore too close to the edge as it may lead to the work piece overhanging.

SANDING BLOCKS

You will need:

- sections of a soft timber or cork. The examples shown were cut from 90 x 30 x 70mm (3 1/12 x 1 1/4 x 2 3/4in) sections

Sandpaper is often considered taboo as far as carving is concerned because of its tendancy, if used incorrectly, to round over the finer details. However, it does play an important role in removing very fine marks that might well end up being exaggerated when polished. If you use sandpaper wrapped around your fingertips, it is possible that any inconsistent lines or surface hollows may only be smoothed rather than completely removed and so the use of shaped sanding blocks is preferable. These can be made very simply from a soft timber or cork and used to give extra precision to the sanding process.

DRILL WITH A NAIL

You will need:

- a suitably sized round nail

Occasionally, a series of tiny round holes are required as part of the carved decoration. I would advise that you avoid using a drill bit, which can often cause splintering on the surface of the timber around the hole.

Remove the head of the nail and round the point over with a file to form a smooth dome. When used in a hand drill, you will find the resulting hole far cleaner. As the hole is burnished rather than cut, it will have a domed bottom and a polished appearance.

Use a nail to drill a clean hole and avoid splintering.

Holding your Work

Carving work that is insufficiently cramped is not only dangerous, but extremely counterproductive. A common problem is often that access is restricted due to the method of cramping being in the way. Outlined below are several ways of cramping different types of work.

G Cramps and Speed Cramps
Among the most commonly used methods of cramping, these can be bought in a variety of sizes and are used to secure carvings to the work surface by compression.

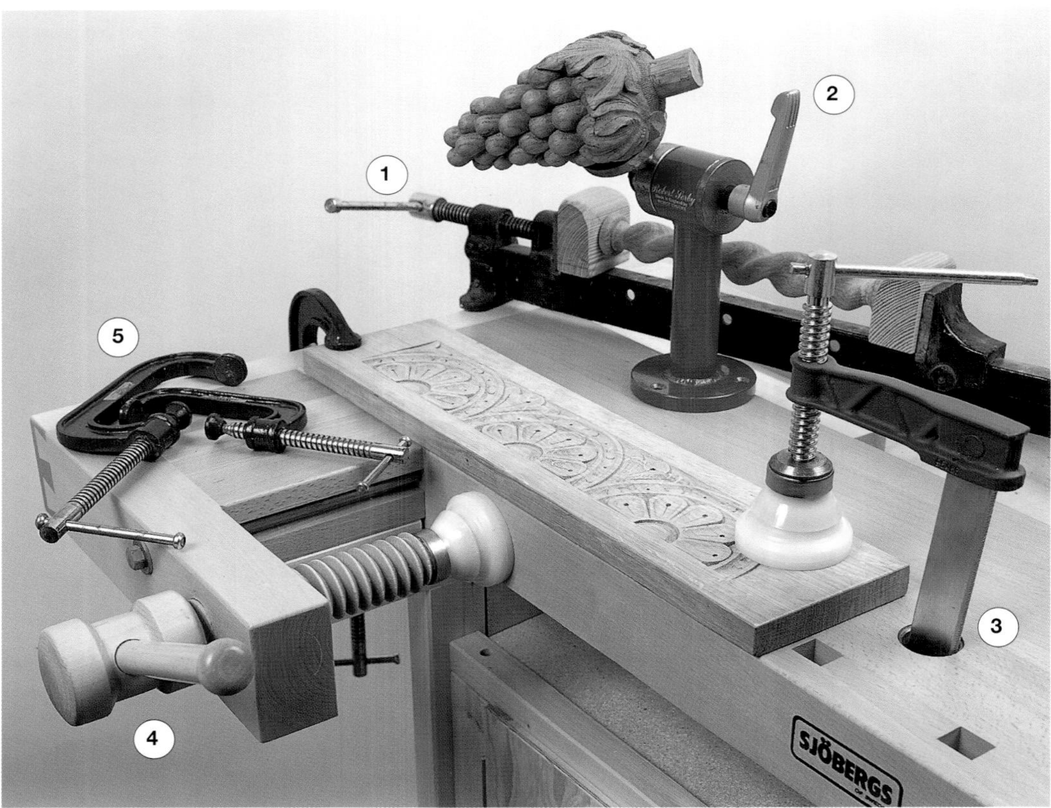

1 Sash cramp
2 Carving cramp
3 Bench holdfast
4 Vice
5 G cramps

Sash Cramps
These can be fixed to the work surface and used rather like a long vice. They are ideal for securing turnings.

Bench Vice
These are strong jaws which can be attached to the workbench. They are designed to hold large sections of timber.

Carving Cramps
There are many variations available although they work on mostly the same principles, forming an

excellent and extremely versatile method of holding. The cramp is secured to the work surface and the carving is fixed, generally by screws, to a manoeuvrable metal plate. This allows the carving to be held firmly in a multitude of different positions.

Bench Screw

The bench screw is basically a threaded bar terminating at a point which screws into the base of the carving. The bar passes through a hole in the work surface and is secured by a large wing nut. Alternatively the bar can pass through a large block of wood which could be secured in the vice.

Bench Holdfast

The bench holdfast passes through a hole in the work surface, cramping the carving from above.

Bench Dogs

These comprise two blocks, one which is fitted in any of a series of holes and protrudes along the bench top, and another which is fitted to the manoeuvrable jaw of the vice. This forms a cramping system for long lengths of timber which need to be held flat against the work surface.

Battens

These are simply lengths of timber which can be nailed or screwed to a board surrounding the carving. This will restrict the movement of the carving and the board can then be secured to the work surface.

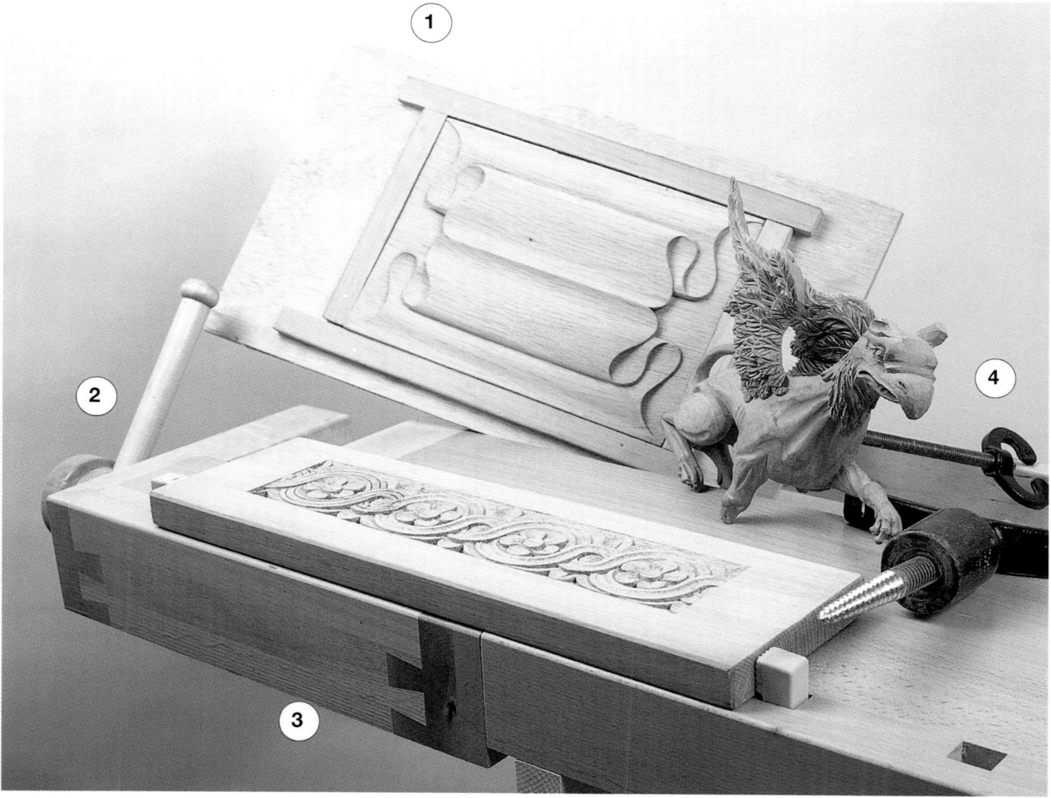

1 Battens
2 Vice
3 Bench dogs
4 Bench screws

Glue

When carving a small object to which access would be severely restricted by clamping, a useful tip is to glue it to a larger board which can be cramped to the work surface.

In order to do this, first ensure that the bottom face of the carving is clean and perfectly flat. 'Key' the surface, by shallowly scoring it with a marking knife to create a checked pattern. Then lightly rub a candle over the surface to apply a thin layer of wax before gluing and cramping the blank to a board. The score marks allow the glue to form a strong bond while the wax provides a barrier between the two surfaces which enables you to release the carving easily on completion.

You could use any sort of glue but PVA (polyvinyl acetate) is ideal. However, if you wish to start work on your carving immediately, you could use a quick-set glue or even a two-part wood filler. The blank should now be secure enough to allow you to carve. On completion, it can be raised using a thin pallet knife (see page 26). Gently work the blade underneath the carving, concentrating on freeing the outer edges before moving to the centre.

After a little persuasion, the carving should lift quite easily, leaving a clean surface to use as a base. It is possible to use paper instead of wax, although this may result in a weaker joint and

The equipment needed for gluing a piece of work to a board to hold it firmly. A thin layer of wax is applied to the back of the piece of work before it is glued to a board which is in turn cramped to the bench top. A pallet knife can be used to lift the project when work is complete.

the back may require more cleaning up. If you do use paper, apply glue to both sides before placing it between the carving blank and the board.

The Workbench or Carver's Stand

The workbench is without doubt one of the carver's most essential aids. It provides the various cramps with a solid base to which you can secure the carving. It is not essential to go to great lengths to buy or make a bench; you just need the surface you are working on to be strong and sturdy. The top should be a suitable thickness to absorb mallet blows, therefore a 50mm (2 in) thick hardwood top with cleated ends would be ideal. However if such a surface is not available, you will find that an old laminated kitchen worktop will be a good substitute. The worktops, which are usually manufactured from a dense chipboard (particle board) or a medium density fibreboard, are not only heavy but also quite strong. It is wise to invert the worktop so that the board is facing uppermost. Once this is done, the board will be kinder to the sharp edges when the chisel blades make contact with the surface. If your workbench has got a sturdy under structure, it is a good idea to allow the top to protrude from between 50-75mm (2-3 in) from the supporting rail. This will make life easier when using G cramps.

Although many carvers choose to be seated whilst working, it is not always practicable and was certainly not permitted while I was training. The bench should be around the same height as the carver's hip bone. This means that the added height will help prevent backache caused through excessive bending after standing and working for prolonged periods. Another method to help avoid bending is to mount your work onto a solid surface which can be pivoted towards you, rather like that of a drawing board. Not all carvings suit being held in this way, but with carvings on panels, for example, this method does allow working with a minimum of physical effort. If you already have a woodworking bench, you could simply make leg extensions which can be removed when not in use. An even simpler option is to raise the bench using a couple of bricks.

If your workspace is restricted, then a carver's stand may be a suitable alternative. This looks very similar to a tall parlour maid's milking stool. It has three legs to prevent rocking on uneven ground which are linked at the bottom by foot rails. The top is usually circular with a hole drilled in it for the benefit of a benchscrew. When the mallet is used or heavy cutting is necessary, the carver applies weight by resting a foot on the lower rails to prevent the stool from moving. Other benches fitted with a seat which use the same weight principles are also popular. They look very similar to a workhorse, at which the carver sits with his work on a raised area in front of him.

Sources of Reference

WORKING FROM ILLUSTRATIONS

Woodcarving beginners and students are often concerned about not being artistic or finding difficulty with drawing. Drawing is a skill that with time, experience and patience will most certainly develop. For the carving by numbers system to work to its fullest potential, it is essential that your carvings are exactly the same dimensions as mine. Each project is purposely designed to fit the profiles of the designated chisel set.

The project plans at the back of this book need to be reconstructed to scale, which is most easily done by enlarging them on a photocopier. The procedure of drawing the design by hand, however, is an important learning process that is as relevant as the carving itself. The reconstruction encourages you to study each area of the design in depth, thus bringing to light important details and requirements that may be overlooked at a glance. As you draw, consider the way in which the high and low areas will be carved.

To start, first draw a grid to the correct scale – in each case one square represents 20mm ($^{25}/_{32}$in). Then copy the design from the grid in the book into the scale size grid you have produced. Rather than trying to transfer the entire design in one go, concentrate on each individual grid square at a time, ensuring the details are reproduced in exactly the same position.

DRAWING ACANTHUS LEAVES

Without doubt the acanthus leaf is the most widely used plant motif in the decorative arts. Its origins lie in the ancient Roman and Greek empires and have been traced back as far as the fifth century BC. The *Acanthus mollis* is a Mediterranean plant which is also known as bears breeches or brank-ursine. It was stylized in different ways for Greek, Roman, Byzantian and Gothic arts but has been in constant use.

During the Renaissance and the revival of classical Roman and Greek decoration, the acanthus leaf returned to its most favoured form and its presence spread wherever European tastes were adopted.

It is good practice to collect pictures of antique furniture and study how the leaf designs have been used. The leaf can often be seen carved in stone to decorate buildings in towns and cities, especially those of the eighteenth century. A photograph of these decorations can prove a valuable source of inspiration when developing designs of your own.

Although the leaf when drawn may look an extremely impressive piece of artwork, it is constructed in a logical series of stages just by following a few simple rules. It is imperative to have an understanding of these basic principles which, in turn, will be replicated in the carvings.

1 The acanthus leaf must first be drawn as a line which will become the centre stem and represent the path that the leaf will follow. This line forms the most important part of the entire illustration with all other lines flowing towards it in a graceful sweep. The acanthus leaf is formed by a series of divisions, the first of which can be seen in Fig. 5, which illustrates the leaf's basic form. The familiar leaf shape is broken down into three divisions which form its essence. Notice how they are proportioned, with the larger division in the centre and the two smaller divisions on either side. Also notice how every single line flows towards this centre line which is absolutely critical for the leaf to appear correct.

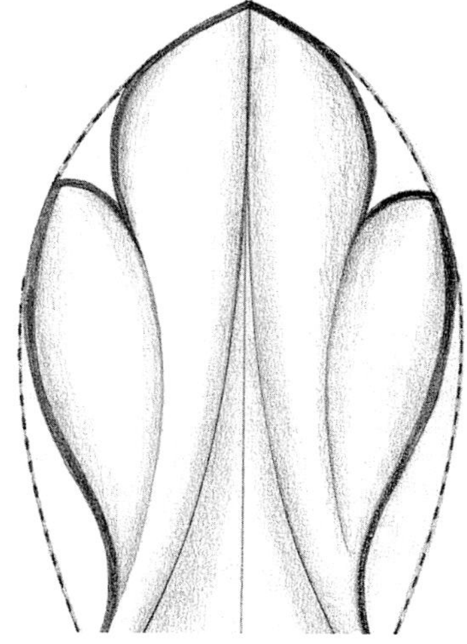

Fig. 5

2 The leaf can be broken into smaller divisions within the confines of the primary shape. Fig. 6 shows that the leaf now comprises seven components. The first and largest section is now divided into three while the smaller divisions on either side have been halved, forming two components. Note that the top leaf should always be made up of three divisions. Once again observe that all lines drawn flow towards that centre line, and the component with three divisions forms a new primary shape

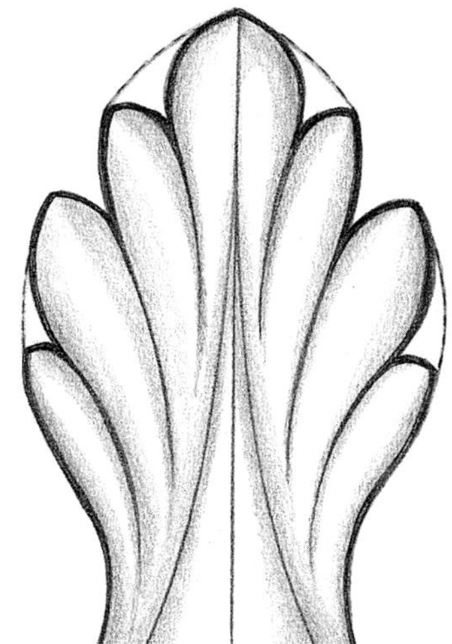

Fig. 6

3 In Fig. 7 you can see the leaf divisions have been broken down once more. The top leaf is divided into three and the two smaller ones on either side are split into two. Note how the new details are drawn internally so as not to alter the basic outside shape. This enables the division to appear visually correct, giving the impression of overlapping components, helping with perspective and giving a three-dimensional look.

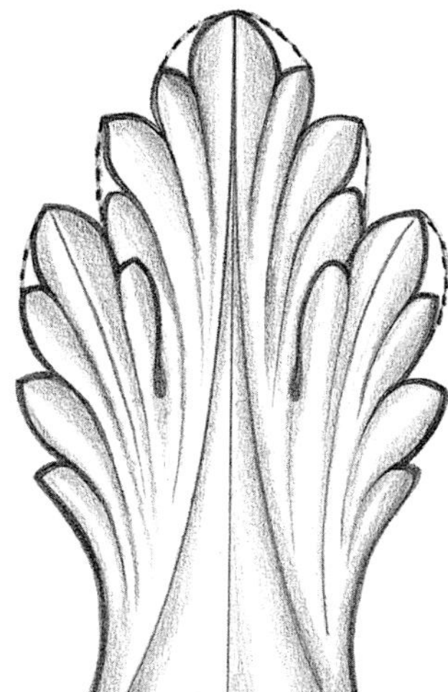

Fig. 7

4 Fig. 8 demonstrates that to create the leaf with many sections divided into sets of three divisions is an attractive option. The basic outside shape is still exactly the same with each internal line flowing towards the centre stem. Each group of three establishes its own primary shape and can be broken down still further if required.

Fig. 8a shows an incorrectly designed leaf. The top leaf has been divided into three and the

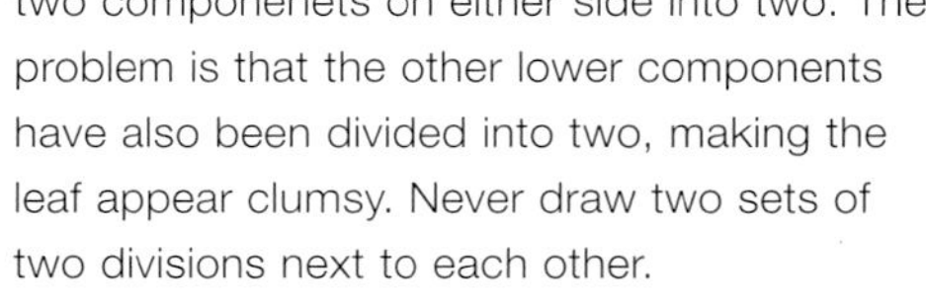

two componenets on either side into two. The problem is that the other lower components have also been divided into two, making the leaf appear clumsy. Never draw two sets of two divisions next to each other.

Always start your design with the centre line (Fig. 9), adding others for more complex leaves. Then fill in the leaf decoration (Fig. 9a), working with the guidelines and remembering that all lines must flow to their central stems.

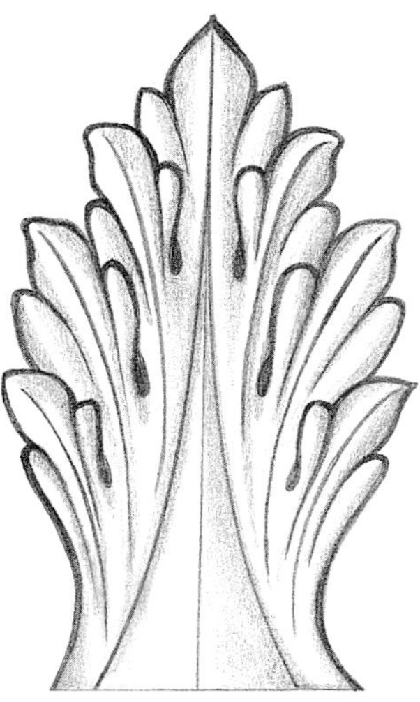

Fig. 8

Fig. 9

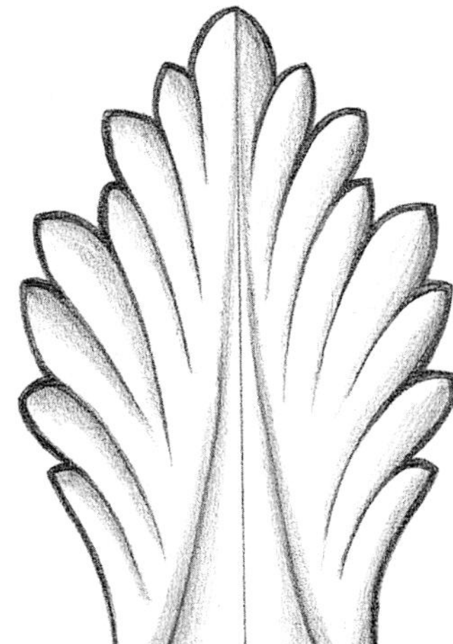

X

Fig. 8a Incorrect leaf divisions.

Fig. 9a

WORKING WITH MODELS

When carving decorations in three dimensions it is often difficult to gauge where the appropriate contours and details should go, especially if you are working from a drawing or photograph. If carving the human figure it is helpful to work with a real model. If this is not feasible, you could use an artist's wooden model. Easily manoeuvrable, they help you to achieve the correct proportions and obtain the right appearance for a sitting or standing figure or a figure in action.

Many projects feature leaves or flowers and you may find it helpful to use fresh ones for inspiration and to experiment with different ways in which they can be arranged. Alternatively you could gather together a collection of attractive or interestingly shaped dried plant material such as rose buds or the poppy seedheads shown below. These can be stored carefully in a box when not in use. To carve fabric as in the linenfold project on page 72, it is useful to have the real thing at hand, especially when carving bows. If the design is large and awkward to arrange, you could try concentrating on small sections at a time. The use of plasticine or clay may prove invaluable when experimenting with detailed forms.

Sources of inspiration.

Carving Techniques

THE CARVING PROCESS

There are four simple stages to any carving project, whether it be chip carving, relief carving or sculpture, and it is essential that each one is completed before the next is undertaken.

Stage 1: Drawing

An outline is all that is initially required. However, time should be taken to get the drawing precise. You would not endeavour to cut a dovetail until it had been correctly marked out.

Stage 2: Construction and Cutting Out

The foundations for the carving are made. If boards need to be glued together to form the required thickness then the joints should be clean. When cutting the carving blank out be as accurate as possible.

Stage 3: Roughing In

The overall shape should now be achieved with the carving chisels. Remove the timber in unwanted areas, defining the high and low levels. It sometimes helps in the early stages to mark the high spots with a cross.

Stage 4: Adding Details

Draw the details on to the 'roughed in' shape. Take your time as it is important here to ensure that the drawing is accurate. The result of the carved detail will be a direct reflection of this.

Remember each stage must be completed before the next is undertaken. It is futile adding details to areas before the entire shape has been formed. After all, you would not ice a cake before you had cooked it.

MARKING OUT TURNINGS

Sometimes it is necessary for turned projects to be marked out into vertical sections, forming a foundation for further marking out to take place. It is imperative that these lines are accurately vertical. If they are slanted, the finished carving will appear to be leaning to one side. A simple technique to aid this marking out process is to fix two nails into the end grain on either end of the turning, making sure they are located exactly in the centres. Then tie a length of thin string around one of the nails (a kite string is ideal). Wrap the other end of the string tightly around the opposite nail so it becomes taught along the length of the blank.

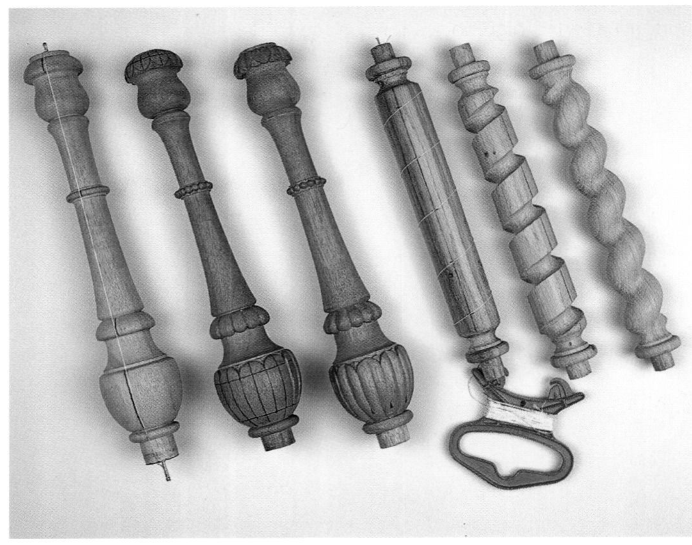

The method for marking out turnings. Left: a candlestick; right: a barley twist.

Next, adjust the string so it appears to divide the turning exactly down the middle and mark this line with a pencil. You should use dividers and mark the appropriate number of divisions around the circumference of the turning, ensuring that they are all perfectly equal. This may take a little time. However, your precision at this stage will be evident in the finished carving. Convert these divisions into vertical lines by moving the string for each division, being diligent about forming a perfect line of symmetry before marking it with a pencil.

This method of marking out is ideal for barley twist carvings. Rather than using the string vertically, use it to wrap around the turning to form the line of the twist. You can adjust the string to ensure all twist divisions are equal and then mark it out with a pencil. The pencil line is then used to form the valley with a rounded surform and the high ridges can be rounded with your chisels.

BACKING OFF

Certain relief carvings and in particular, three-dimensional carvings, often require all surplus timber to be removed, a process known as 'backing off'. The example in the photograph shows this technique being carried out on the wing of the griffin. On the right you will also see an example of eighteenth century carved leaf work that appears to be extremely delicate. However, as a result of the backing off being carried out correctly, the carving is surprisingly strong.

This process is carried out by placing the carving upside down on an old cushion or material so as not to damage the surface details. Hold the carving securely with one hand and using chisel No. 1, carefully remove any surplus timber that was not previously accessible. Remember always to cut away from the hand holding the carving and only remove tiny slithers of timber at a time with the minimum of force. Obviously this process can be extremely hazardous, so make sure you are in control of the chisel at all times – one slip could lead to a nasty cut.

The general idea is to remove timber without making the carving too weak. In the photograph below only the very tips of the carvings have been reduced to a fine point, with the bulk of timber remaining out of sight.

Backing off. Notice how delicate the wing appears from the front. The leaves on the right are examples of eighteenth century carvings showing how backing off produces very fine edges.

Finishing and Ageing Methods

FINISHING

There is a wide range of finishes available and only by experimenting will you find one that suits your needs. However, in spite of the different effects you can achieve and the slight variations in terms of application, there is a fairly standard approach to the finishing process and outlined below are a few general guidelines which should be taken into consideration.

PREPARATION

The use of sand paper is often frowned upon as, used incorrectly, it does tend to round over sharp edges and crisp lines which have been painstakingly strived for. This can be avoided, however, by using sanding blocks (see page 29). It is absolutely imperative that when using carving chisels the maximum effort is made to achieve a fine finish before you even consider applying a wax, polish or stain, but sandpaper is useful for smoothing the overall surface and removing tiny tool marks and scratches which when polished, become exaggerated. When sanding I would rarely use anything coarser than 120 grit and usually finish off with 1200 grit. All traces of dust and loose fibres must then be gently removed with a clean nail brush.

STAINING

If you wish to stain the carving you must be aware that the stain will be absorbed at different rates as a result of the diverse amounts of exposed end grain. This will obviously present you with an uneven distribution of colour, which is intensified with softwoods or if quantities of stain collect in inaccessible crevices. Although it is a factor which must be taken into

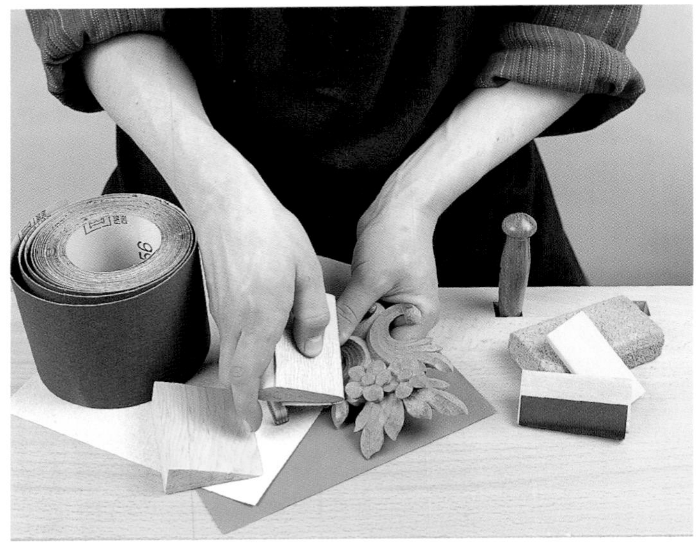

Using a sanding block to smooth the surfaces without rounding over the edges.

Applying a wood stain with a brush.

consideration, when polished it often appears quite attractive, adding depth and perspective to the carving. I would, therefore, strongly recommend that you consider the suitability of the stain for the job and most importantly always try it out on a piece of scrap timber first.

The grain should not be raised as this will only lead to further use of abrasive papers or wire wool. Water-based stains should therefore be avoided, with spirit and oil based stains making better choices. Apply the stains liberally with a brush to ensure that all areas are covered. Then with a cloth remove the surplus and allow the stain to dry.

POLISHING

Whichever polish you decide to use, whether the timber has been pre-stained or not, it is sensible to avoid the thicker polishes. The general rule is that the polish should not appear any thicker than water. If it does, it should be thinned. I find that most shellac-based products, for example button polish, transparent polish and sanding sealer are excellent because of their quick drying characteristics. Ensure that the timber is free from all traces of dust and unwanted marks. Using a good quality brush or polisher's mop, apply the polish sparingly, as it is essential to prevent it from running or collecting in any recesses. Remember, three thin coats are better than one thick one! Usually after approximately four or five coats, a sufficient sheen has developed which, after drying, can be cut back or de-nibbed using grade 0000 wire wool. Rub the polish very gently until all traces of shine have been removed to form a very smooth matt surface.

On polished wood the amount of light reflected from the surface determines the degree of shine. If you were to examine various objects under a microscope you would find that those formed by closely connected molecules tend to be the most reflective. You will also find that the smoother the object, the more intense the reflection. Timber in its natural form can be compared to a bundle of drinking straws, the holes representing the end grain and the length of the straws forming the long grain. The very nature of polish is that its molecules are more densely packed than those of timber. Therefore when applied to the surface of a piece of wood it enhances the sheen. (Think of a table top or a piano which has been French polished for example.) However, before the polish is applied, the timber must be carefully prepared to a fine finish as a smooth surface will allow you to achieve a greater quality of sheen. The surface of the timber across long grain is made up of closely knitted tubes which form a series of ridges and valleys. When the polish is applied, it coats the entire surface, not only filling the valleys, but also making the ridges higher. It is common practice to cut back the polish using very fine abrasive paper between coats. This helps to reduce the height of the ridges, allowing the valleys to reach the same level which in turn forms an entirely flat surface and gives a brighter sheen.

Denibbing

After the polish has been carefully and evenly applied, it should be allowed to cure. Even when using thinner polishes, which in general dry more quickly than thicker, it is wise to leave them overnight. When dry, the polished surface may feel slightly gritty as a result of small particles of dust in the atmosphere settling on it. This can be remedied by using 0000 grade wire wool to reduce the overall sheen to a dull matt finish. However, make sure that the polish is only dulled and not removed. A cotton bud can often help to work the wire wool into smaller crevices.

WAXING

Finally, apply a coat of paste wax polish, which is available in a range of complementary timber colours. It should be applied with a soft brush to ensure that the wax is distributed into the smaller and more awkward recesses. A tooth brush is particularly useful for this purpose. Then, after a short drying time, it can be buffed with a soft cloth to produce a deep and lasting shine. If the carving is to be located outdoors then a water resistant finish is required and, therefore, a wax finish will be unsuitable. Many of the exterior finishes tend to be thicker, so make sure you thin them down before applying them.

Applying wax with a toothbrush.

AGEING TECHNIQUES

Occasionally it is desirable for a carving to take on an antique look, enabling it to blend into its intended surrounding decor. It is fairly common to hear of craftspeople 'distressing' furniture using chains and nails to create random dents and scratches, thus creating the illusion of many years of wear and tear. Although chains and nails are rather brutal for carving, there are a number of other ways to create this appearance. Ageing techniques obviously vary according to the type of timber. However, there are three main factors which can help you to produce an aged effect.

TIMBER CHOICE

More often than not the backs of old carvings have become very dirty and grey with age. One of the most sensible ways to replicate this appearance is to use old timber. Quite often it will have an old, dirty surface which has occurred naturally. By keeping one face of the timber unplaned you will have an authentic aged back for the carving. Another important consideration when using old timber is that it will be extremely well seasoned and is quite likely to have deep splits and shakes. These features can also contribute to the antique look.

A collection of seventeenth century carvings and an example of an aged piece of timber planed on one side.

DISTRESSING

There are many products on the market which can change the colour of timber, whether it is to make it darker with stains or to lighten it with A and B bleach. You should experiment with these products on a piece of scrap timber as there are few set rules.

Carving is an art form which naturally attracts admiring hands. Of course, many years of admiration as well as day-to-day knocks and scrapes will give the carving a rounded appearance, producing a shine on its most accessible areas. This can be replicated by rubbing the high spots of a new piece of work with a smooth hard object, such as a piece of metal, a stone or a burnisher as shown in the photograph below. The rubbing action creates burnished areas and also helps to round over prominent edges. A medium grade wire wool will also create this burnished effect.

APPLYING THE FINISH

As already described, certain areas of a carving are bound to suffer greater wear than others, producing variations of colour. On a new piece of work, which you want to take on an antique appearance or which needs to blend with an old carving, colour variations can be exaggerated after toning the carving with stains or bleach by rubbing the highlights with fine wire wool. This process will remove some of the colour, also leaving a polished sheen. Following this, polishes may be added, or if a deep, subtle lustre is required, a paste wax can be applied directly on to the bare timber.

Using a burnisher on a wooden panel.

PROJECTS

Basic Flower

This is a very simple project which would be appropriate for the centre of a small box lid or, used as a repetitive motif, as a decorative border. It provides a good practice piece, allowing you to familiarize yourself with the chisel techniques, and it is easily made smaller or larger depending on your requirements. I suggest starting with a piece of suitable timber (see page 17) at least 100 x 80 x 12mm (4 x 3 ⅛ x ½in). Plane the surface flat and secure it to the work surface (see pages 30–33).

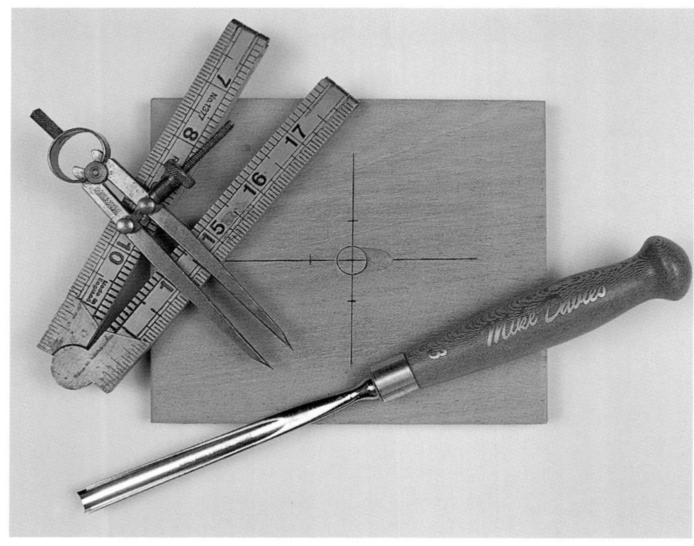

1 Using chisel No. 3 held vertically in the pinch position, gently set in a cut in the centre of the board. Adjust the position of the chisel and set in further cuts with the cutting edge to form a complete circle. Pencil in a cross through the centre of the circle, one line running with the grain and the other against it. With a pair of dividers, mark two points on each line 10mm (⅜in) from the outside edge of the circle. With chisel No. 3 in the fist position, place the centre of the cutting edge on to either of the marks on the line running with the grain and gently slide it towards the circle to remove a scoop of wood. Set the circle in deeper and repeat until you reach a depth of approximately 5mm (3⁄16in) where the petal meets the circle.

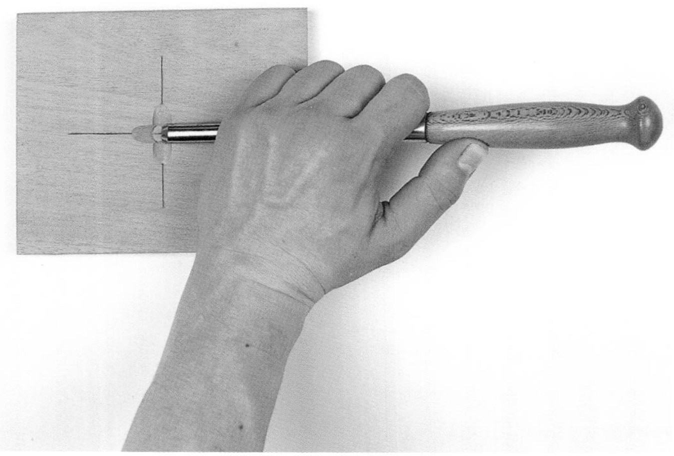

2 Using your other hand, repeat this process on the same line, working from the opposite mark. Form the third and fourth petals working from the marks on the line pencilled across the grain. Next, round over the circle in the centre by holding chisel No. 3 in the fist position and inverting it so that the convex side is uppermost. Place the cutting edge on the widest part of the circle. Working with the grain, tap the chisel from the centre of the circle to the outside edge. As you reach the outside edge, raise the angle of the chisel.

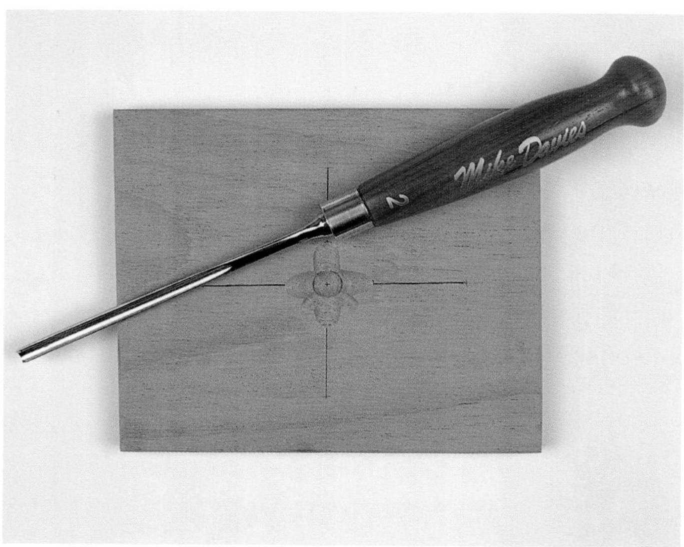

3 Having completed the other side of the button using the opposite hand, you can then work on rounding it over smoothly.

Next select chisel No. 2 to form the smaller petals located between the larger ones. You may need to spend a little more time perfecting the shape of each petal, so that they are more clearly defined by the appearance of small ridge lines. Try to ensure that the flower is symmetrical, with each of the petals exactly opposite its counterpart.

4 Finally, clean up any remaining pencil marks by giving the panel a light sand. Once you have finished the flower you may wish to wax or stain it (see pages 40–42) to give the wood added richness and depth.

Having mastered the techniques for carving this simple decoration, you can now create a whole range of other traditional designs. 'Fluting' for example is done just by elongating the petal shapes shown here. Why not experiment to develop other forms of decoration that can be achieved using these basic cuts?

Berry Moulding

The berries are carved on to an astragal-shaped moulding (see Figs. 12 and 13a, page 107) which can be applied to numerous items of wooden furnishing including the glazing bars of a door or the moulding around the edge of a box or table. This decoration can even be carved on turnings, as seen in the candlestick project.

Carving berries is an excellent learning exercise because the element of repetition means that the techniques required soon become second nature.

1 Form the moulding along the edge of a plank held in the vice. On completion of the berries, cut the plank down to the required size. If you have a moulding plane or router, cutters are available to enable you to cut an astragal moulding of the right size. First remember to scribe a line where the cut separating the moulding from the plank will be made around 2mm (1⁄16in) below the shoulder.

Holding chisel No. 2 in the pinch position, form a circle on a piece of scrap wood. Set the dividers with the points resting in the grooves at the full diameter of the circle (8mm (5⁄16in)). Then mark a series of divisions along the upper ridge of the moulding.

2 Hold chisel No. 1 in the pinch position and rest the blade on top of the first division. Start a dividing cut with the heel of the chisel by rolling the blade over the rounded ridge. Re-adjust the chisel's position so the cut may be completed with the pointed tip, ensuring that you do not mark the moulding's shoulders. Apply gentle controlled pressure and continue this action down the length of the moulding.

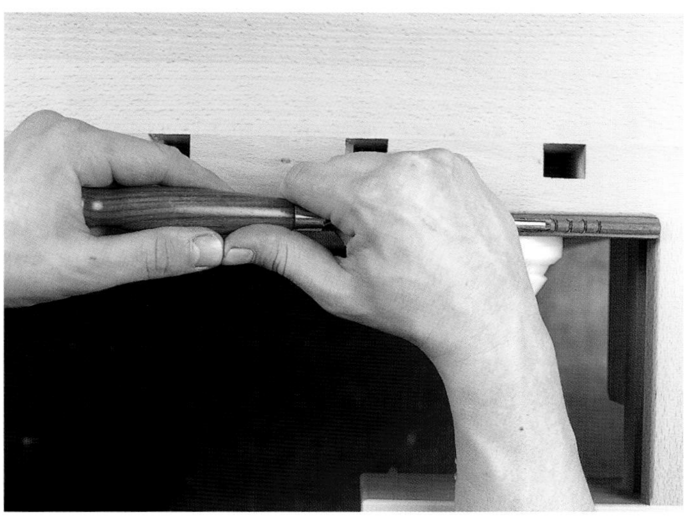

3 Hold chisel No. 2 in the fist position, form an anchor and place the inner cutting edge of the chisel between two cuts in the centre of a division. Apply slight pressure and ease the chisel down towards the division cut line to form one side of the berry. Practise raising the handle and work the blade through the wood in a fluid motion, creating half the berry in one cut. Repeat this for each division. Using the other hand (see Becoming Ambidextrous, page 14), follow the same procedure to complete the second half of each berry.

4 On completion of the moulding, perfect the appearance of the individual berries by setting their profiles in a little deeper with chisel No. 2 and generally tidying up any lumps and bumps. Use chisel No. 1 to remove any surplus timber and splinters still attached around the base of the berries. A light sanding may now be appropriate, although avoid altering the overall shape.

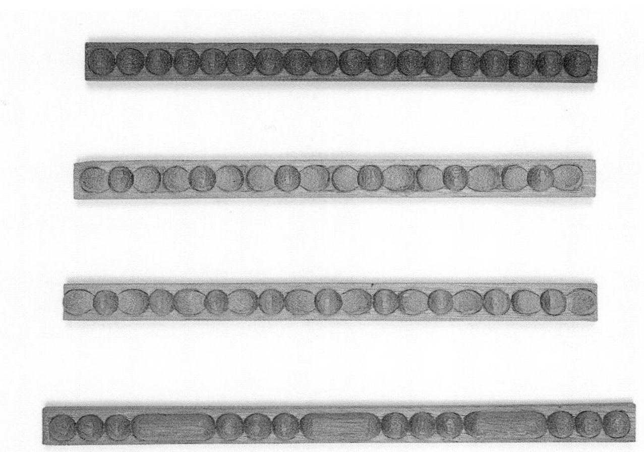

5 Give the work a light rub with a clean dry nail brush to remove any remaining splinters. Here you can see both the finished berry moulding (top) and variations of the decoration which can be carved into the same dimensions of moulding. Why not try your hand at these, referring to Figs. 13b–d on page 107?

For the moulding shown here I used a Brazilian mahogany. As it is designed to be applied to furniture etc. a matching timber is usually chosen for a moulding, although a contrast might be an interesting option.

Waterleaf Moulding

The origins of this versatile moulding decoration lie in the classical architecture of ancient Rome and Greece. It can be used as edging around table tops or boxes, for cornice mouldings at the top of furniture or for plinths surrounding the base and to decorate turnings and mouldings for glazing bars. The moulding is made to standard dimensions and cutters of the appropriate size can be purchased for routers or spindle moulders. It can also be formed by hand, using a rebate plane to set in the shoulders and a chisel or scratch stock to round the quadrant. I chose Brazilian mahogany although most dense, close grained timbers would be suitable.

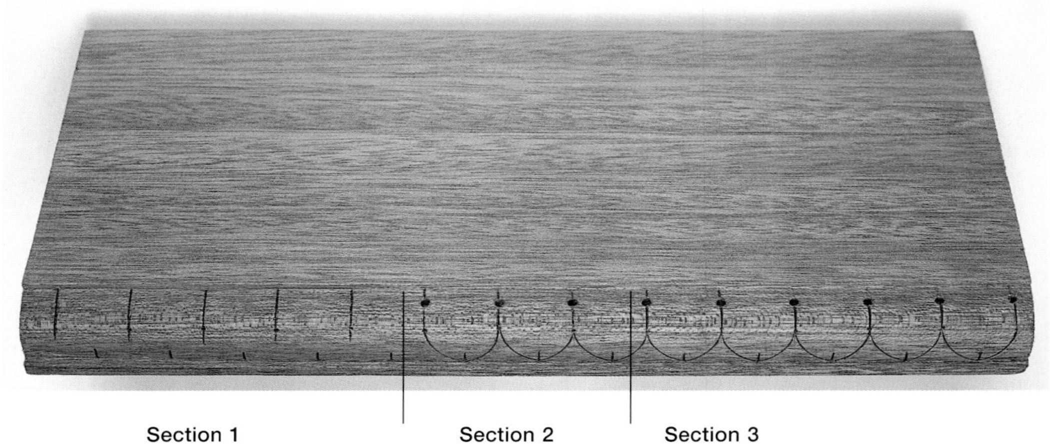

Section 1 Section 2 Section 3

Section 1 Referring to Fig. 15c page 108, mark a series of division lines, exactly 18mm (23⁄32in) apart, from the top of the quadrant down to the centre. Use a pair of dividers for accuracy. Then mark another set of equally spaced divisions along the bottom of the moulding, exactly between the first.

Section 2 Holding chisel No. 4 in the pinch position, gently set in the profile of the leaves using the full shape of the cutting edge. Place one point of the cutting edge on the bottom division line and the other point on the corresponding top division line where it stops half-way down the moulding. Ensure that the cut is set in at a 90° to the surface of the timber. You have now formed half the waterleaf shape. Repeat this process along the entire length of the moulding and then work in the opposite direction to complete the second half of the leaves.

Next, create a series of holes 2mm (1⁄16in) in diameter (see page 29) to form eyelets. The holes should be located on the top division lines, exactly 4mm (5⁄32in) down from the upper shoulder. Gauge this distance using your dividers.

Section 3 Use chisel No. 1 to complete the shape of the leaves by gently setting in a series of straight lines from the holes to the points where the two cuts made by chisel No. 4 meet. Apply light pressure at this stage to mark the surface.

Section 4 Section 5

Section 4 With chisel No. 1, elongate each hole to form a teardrop. A shaped punch is extremely useful for definition, but you must cut the wood first rather than simply punching the shape on to the surface, which will bruise the surrounding area. Next, set your dividers to 7mm (9/32in) and mark a series of divisions between the holes, at the top of the leaves as shown.

Section 5 With chisel No. 1, make two diagonal cuts for each leaf running from the 7mm (9/32in) division marks down to the bottom centre line. This will form a series of elongated V shapes as you can see here. Use gentle pressure as this forms an area of short grain between the cuts which can easily chip out.

Section 6 Section 7 Section 8

Section 6 Holding chisel No. 4 in the fist position, begin to round the leaves down towards the centre lines. Cut the centre lines a little deeper as you progress so that the waste timber can be removed. Stand centrally in front of your work, holding the chisel in the left hand to carve towards the left-hand side of the bench and vice versa for the right.

Section 7 Now, using chisel No. 1, form a line running down the centre of each of the narrow triangular shapes formed in step 5. Cut this carefully and slice down towards it on either side, forming a V-shaped valley. Always try to ensure that all cuts are clean and free from splinters.

Section 8 Still using chisel No. 1, continue to carve away wood from each of these central sections to form a series of elongated pyramid shapes. Then mark a series of vertical pencil lines along the bottom of the moulding, between the larger leaves, exactly opposite the row of teardrop-shaped holes above.

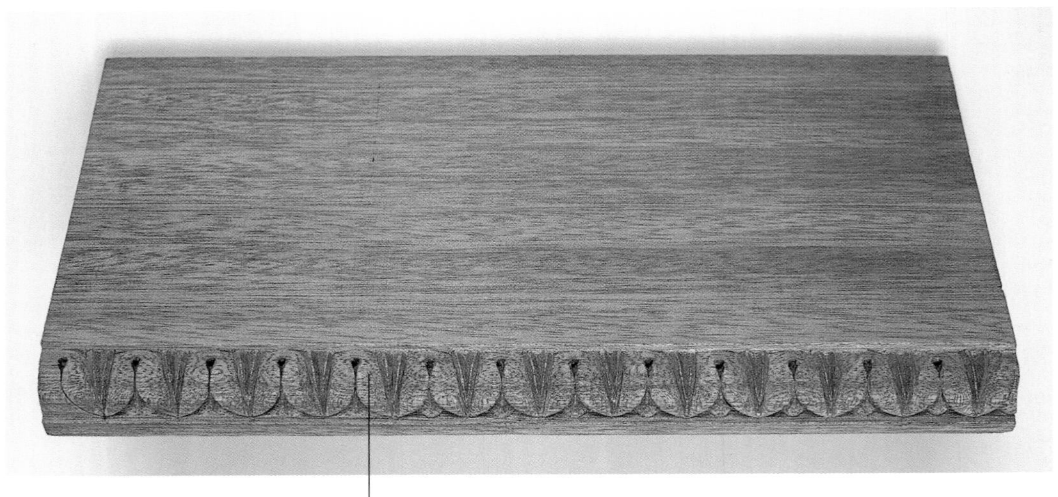

Section 9

Section 10

Section 9 Use chisel No. 3 to slice a small amount of wood away from one side of these centre lines, working towards the edges of the leaves. Remove just a fraction at a time, setting in the profile line of each leaf a little deeper as you progress. Continue this process until the leaves have around 2mm (1⁄16in) of definition. Now with your opposite hand, repeat the procedure but in the other direction, forming a series of ridges in place of the pencil marks.

Section 10 Using chisel No. 2, set in the shape of the smaller leaves between the larger ones as shown and remove the waste with chisel No. 1. Finally, use a clean, dry nail brush to remove any loose fibres.

Fig. 15b on page 108 illustrates a rather more simplistic version of the waterleaf. It follows the same procedures and dimensions, except that the central vein is absent.

Egg and Dart Moulding

Pictured opposite (underneath the finished waterleaf moulding) is an 'Egg and Dart' moulding. Also known as 'Egg and Tongue' or 'Egg and Anchor' it can be carved into the same dimensions of quadrant moulding. Its origins are Greek and, like many other classical designs, it has now become a popular form of neo-classical decoration incorporated into architecture and world furnishing. The egg and dart moulding requires virtually the same techniques as the waterleaf project and the use of chisel Nos. 1, 2, 3 and 4. Refer to Fig. 15a on page 108 when marking out the moulding and gauging the proportions.

Flat Carving

This particular style of carving, known as 'flat carving', is commonly found decorating furniture from the Jacobean period (1603–1688). The designs are varied and although sometimes of a simplistic appearance, they can enhance oak furniture tremendously. The basis of flat carving is that areas of wood are reduced from the surface to leave a pattern in the remaining timber. You will find a number of other flat carving designs included in the Ideas section towards the back of the book (see pages 124–137).

The appearance of the finished carving will benefit if the top surface of the pattern remains perfectly flat and if the design is crisp without any of the signs of rounding caused by the bevel of the chisels. Make sure your chisels are properly sharpened so that you can make clean and accurate cuts and clear away any splinters as you work. It will also help if the cuts around the outside edge are set in at 90° to the surface of the timber.

Stage 1

Stage 1 Photocopy or redraw Fig. 16 on page 109 to scale and make a stencil from stiff card. The stencil can then be used to produce a repetitive design as shown above. Ensure that the selected piece of timber is planed flat and sanded smooth before marking the design on to the surface. I recommend using oak for this particular project although chestnut, ash or elm would make equally suitable alternatives.

Note the straight lines which form a box around the design. This box should be centrally located on the surface of the timber surrounded by a border which should be left undecorated.

Stage 2

Stage 3

Stage 2 Next set in cuts over the pencil lines using the various chisels from your set. Use chisel No. 1 to set in the straight lines. Start the cut with the heel then introduce the tip in a guilloteen motion. Make a series of cuts with the length of the chisel's cutting edge rather than one long one.

Stage 3 To bring the design to life, carve towards the set in cuts at an angle, making sure of course that you carve on the outside of the pattern. Try to maintain the same angle of cut throughout. Where two defining cuts meet back to back a ridge line will form, which will sometimes be below the surface. To carve away the timber in the scroll shape area, first carve towards the tip of the leaf with chisel No. 2, forming a scoop and then work around the rest of the area with chisel No. 1.

Stage 4

Stage 4 After completing the outer edges of the design, ensuring that the cuts are at right angles to the surface of the timber, you can proceed with the internal detail. With chisel No. 2 set in the four circles, again at 90° and remove a little surrounding timber from each at an angle. Next, concentrate on the crescent-shaped decorations located on the side leaves of each fleur-de-lis. Using chisel No. 3 set in a 90° cut on the curved line closest to the scroll shape. Then complete the shape with a second cut sliced towards the first at an angle. On each of the central leaves, make two incisions with chisel No. 4 at angles towards each other so that they meet and form a straight line along the bottom. Form the small holes in the centre of the border decorations between the fleurs-de-lis using a rotating nail in a drill (see page 29). Finally, sand the work gently.

Page 125 shows a similar design but with the background decorated using a textured punch (see pages 25–6) to create tiny indentations.

Guilloche

'Guilloche', a French term, describes a decoration used widely in ancient Greece and Rome and which is particularly evident on the architecture of both these civilizations. The design comprises two or more bands interwoven to form a repetative pattern which is interspersed on occasions with other designs such as flowers. The same basic elements of the guilloche also featured prominently in Celtic, Anglo Saxon and early Scandinavian decorative arts, producing in some cases extremely elaborate and complex patterns. The guilloche was also used extensively in Islamic and Moorish artwork and was refined extensively during the Renaissance, drawing on classical, medieval and Moorish influences. The results of this development became evident on furniture dating from the sixteenth century onwards. At first, it was simply carved. However, it was later painted and inlayed into the fine furnishings of the Georgian period.

As mentioned, the guilloche decoration can be found in many different guises, but the continuous configuration of interwoven bands remains the ruling principle. It can be used to decorate rails, mouldings, or even panels.

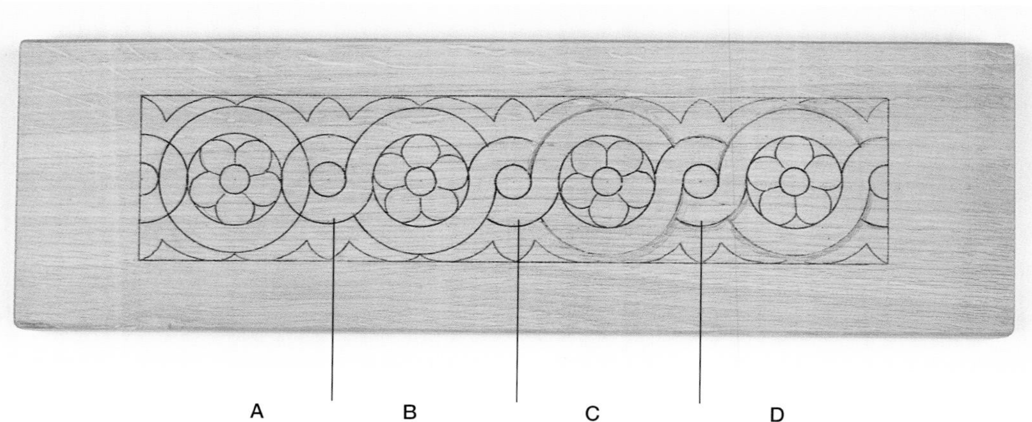

Stages A-D Photocopy or redraw the design to scale referring to Fig. 17 on page 110. It is advisable to use a compass to form the circles. Once the drawing is accurately reproduced, you could make a stencil, which will help for marking long lengths of the repetitive design (see page 27). In section A you will see the required markings on the timber. In section B note how certain sections of the circles have been erased, producing the continuous over and under configuration of the interwoven bands.

Section C shows how the outside perimeter of the largest circle has been defined. Select chisel

No. 5 for this purpose and very carefully carve the edges at 90°. Stop the cut on one side where it meets the outside of the smaller circle and on the other where it meets the inner berry. Make sure you do not overstep the mark here as a mistake at this stage would be extremely difficult to correct.

Now develop the smaller circle as shown in section D. Place the cutting edge of chisel No. 4 on the circle, ensuring that the blade is vertical to the timber's surface. Now set in the profile by gently tapping the handle with a mallet to create a shallow incision. Remove the chisel, reposition it and take a further cut towards the circle at a slight angle to the incision. The result should be the removal of a tiny segment which gives the circle greater definition. You may need to repeat this procedure until you reach the required depth of around 2–3mm (1⁄16–1⁄8in).

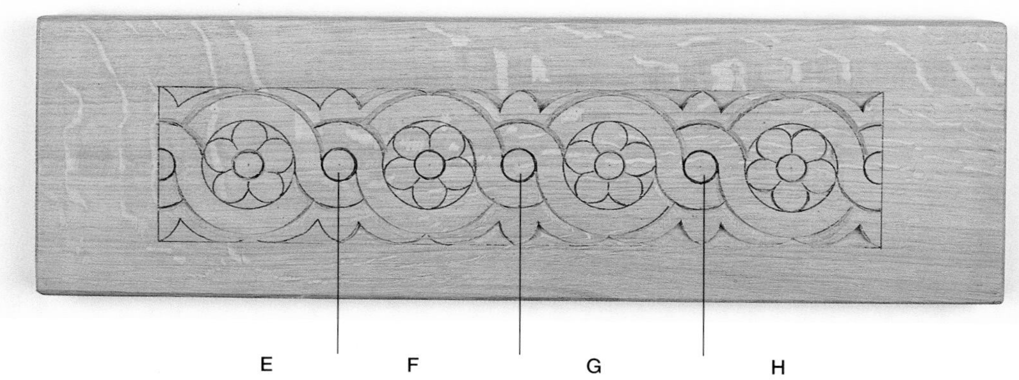

Stages E-H Now set in the smallest inner circles as shown in section E. Then select chisel No. 4 to set in the profiles of the leaf shapes at the top and bottom of the design. This stage can be seen in section F. Define the outside leaves by removing the surrounding timber. This process will also define the edge of the border. Chisel No. 4, though it may not seem the obvious tool to use, is most appropriate for this task. Clearing the waste should be done using two directions of cut. Carve towards the left for the left-hand side of each leaf and vice versa for the right (see Becoming Ambidextrous, page 14) to form a high central ridge. Then carve the ridge away using the square end of the chisel blade to get to the point where the two leaf components meet. Chisel No. 1 is also useful for clearing the waste in this awkward place. Take extra care not to carve over the border line by mistake. It is important that it appears as crisp and straight as possible. The required outcome can be seen in section G. Next set in the flower petals with vertical cuts from chisel No. 3 as shown in section H.

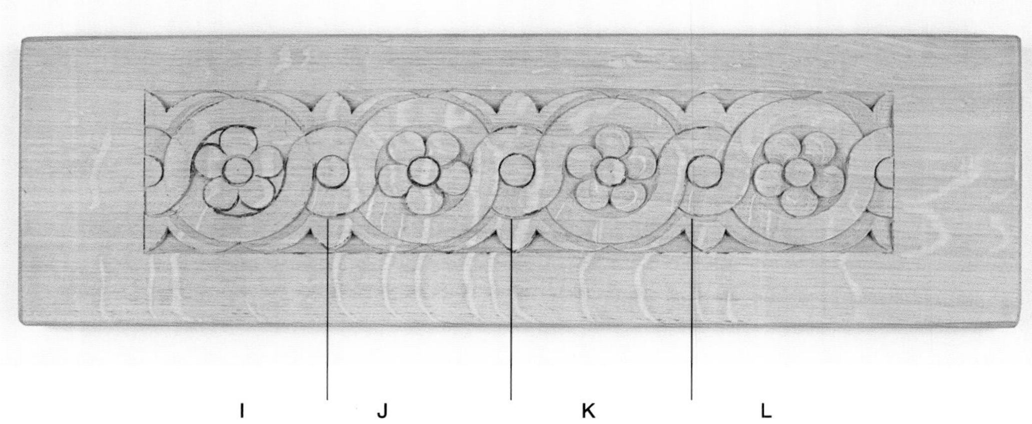

Stages I-L Shape the bands to create the essential interwoven pattern seen in section I. Use chisel No. 1 or, alternatively, a 13mm (½in) flat bevel edge chisel for this purpose. The edges of the weave should be cut to a depth of around 2–3mm (1⁄16–⅛in) at their lowest point.

Section J shows the next step. Define the flower petals with chisel Nos. 4 and 1 by carefully removing the wood from the area surrounding each one. The procedure is the same as that used for the leaf shapes along the border.

Use chisel No. 4 to define the petals further as shown in section K. Make a single cut for each petal, setting in the curved cutting edge of the chisel in a uniform direction. A slicing cut should then be made on the right-hand side of each incision to produce a fan-like appearance. Select chisel No. 3 and take a small scoop out of each petal towards the flower centre.

Now finish shaping the leaves. In section L you will see how the curved shape of each leaf has been carved down towards the perimeter of the larger circle with chisel No. 1. The centre leaves should then be carved gradually down towards the edges of the smaller circles with chisel No. 3.

Note

For this design I recommend using a piece of oak measuring 450 x 150 x 20 (14 x 6 x ¾in). This is the timber traditionally used for this style of carving. However, ash or elm would be just as appropriate. As you can see, oak is a fairly pale wood so you may wish to stain it deeper (see Finishing Methods, pages 40–42). Once you have tried this design, why not use a different type of wood or a decorative finish on the guilloche variation shown on page 127?

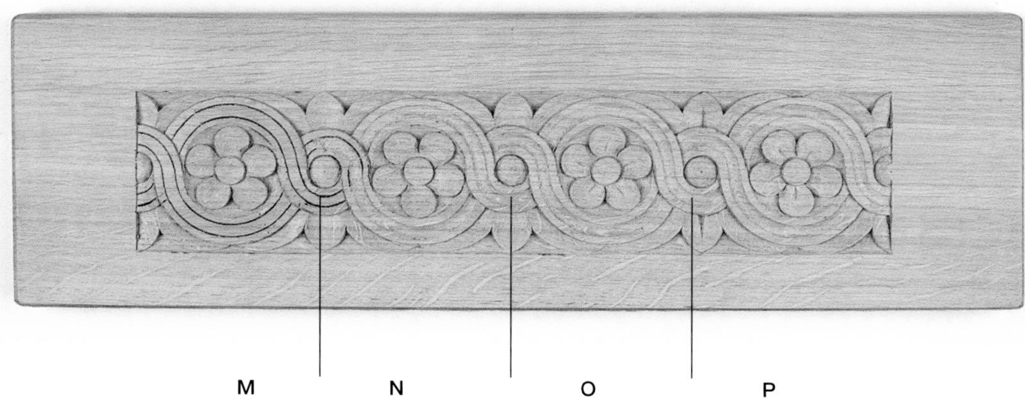

Stages M-P You will now need to mark more detail on to the design as shown in section M. You can use a compass for accurate marking, but avoid pressing too hard or you will risk making deep holes with the point. Section M also shows the development of the centre berries which are encircled by the bands. They are rounded over with chisel No. 4, which should also be used to remove a slight scoop from the surface of the circle in the centre of each flower, creating a dished effect. Take this opportunity to remove any marks left by the compass.

Following your pencil lines, carve a channel into each band using chisel No. 2. These channels enhance the interwoven effect (section N). Try to keep the ridge lines as clean and flowing as possible without forming any unwanted 'elbows'. Remember to slide your chisels (page 13) to maximize the effectiveness of the cutting edges. This is especially relevant at this stage here as you will unavoidably meet areas of awkward grain.

To add the finishing touches, as shown in section O, use chisel No. 5 to form small veins on each flower petal and also on the centre leaves of the peripheral decoration.

It may be necessary to give the work a light sanding to remove pencil marks (section P). However, leaving a few remaining tool marks may give the project a more authentic look as carvings from this period were relatively unsophisticated.

Patera

Paterae are popular forms of decoration with a multitude of uses. They stem from classical architecture and were later used to decorate furniture. A suggested application would be to set them into the legs of tables and chairs. However, on their own they also make interesting gifts. Paterae can be made in many different shapes and sizes. Once you have mastered this one, why not try designing your own? The project incorporates skills learned from the berry and waterleaf mouldings which will be required to form the flower centre and the petals.

1 Cut out a blank of the dimensions given in Fig. 18 on page 111. Then glue the blank to a board following the detailed instructions on page 32. Once the glue is dry, you can then clamp the board to your work surface, ensuring that the grain runs horizontally in front of you as shown here. You are now ready to start the shaping process.

2 Use chisel No. 4 to shape the blank, leaving the edge square and approximately 4mm (⅛in) deep. Form the dome with chisel No. 1, holding it in the 'fist' position and using the tapping technique. You may also find it useful to refer to Cutting Directions on page 15. Any imperfections can now be smoothed away with sandpaper. You may wish to use a lathe to reach this stage if you have access to one.

3 Use chisel No. 3 to set in a circle 13mm (½in) in diameter in the centre of the dome. Carve away the wood to form a dish shape 25mm (1in) in diameter, around the central circle, at a depth of roughly 6mm (¼in). Leave the inner circle untouched at this stage.

To form the petals, mark eight divisions around the circumference of the flower with dividers and a pencil. Divide the sections once again and draw straight lines through the centre of the disk to link each of the new marks. This will give you sixteen separate divisions, evenly spaced, eight of which are linked by lines.

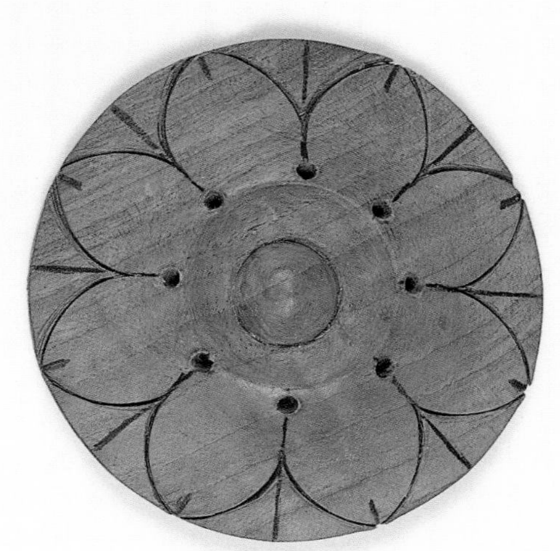

4 Round over the centre button with chisel No. 3. You may need to deepen the dish around it a little more. Try the tapping technique and remember to use the right hand to carve to the right of the bench and vice versa for the left (see page 14).

Next drill a series of 2mm (1⁄16in) holes to form the eyelets of the flower, using the method shown on page 29. The holes should be located on your long dividing lines exactly 15mm (⅝) from the centre. Form the outline of the petals using chisel No. 4 by setting in shallow cut lines, linking the short marks to the longer lines.

Note

For this particular style of patera I chose walnut as it is relatively easy to work. The wood is also an attractive mid-brown colour which complements most pieces of traditional furniture. However, as you can see from the many different designs shown on page 63, it is possible to choose from a wide range of woods the one most suited to your purposes. The appearance of the patera can be dramatically transformed simply by selecting a dark or pale wood or one with an interesting grain pattern.

5 Carve a little wood away from either side of the pencil lines that fall between the petals, forming central ridges and making the petal shapes prominent. Then extend the drill holes into teardrop shapes with chisel No. 1. Point them down towards the petals using a punch to define the shape further (see page 25). Now cut a shallow dividing line down the middle of each petal using chisel No. 1. Make sure this line radiates accurately from the centre of the flower.

6 Use chisel No. 4 to hollow each petal from the outside edges down towards the centre line, forming a V shape with rounded sides. As you work, gradually deepen the centre cuts with chisel No. 1.

Use chisel No. 3 to shape the small petals, which are located between the larger ones. Cut along the outside edge of each small petal from the central ridge down towards the larger petals in an arc shape on both sides, creating a more pointed tip. Complete this shaping process with a number of small cuts to avoid splitting the larger petals.

7 With chisel No. 4 round the shoulders over the eyelets down towards the centre cut lines on the larger petals. Continue to deepen the central line on each petal with controlled cuts. Try to achieve a consistent depth with all the petals. Now ease a pallet knife underneath the completed flower, freeing the edges first. After releasing the flower, scrape the base with a flat chisel to remove any remaining traces of glue or wax. You can now back off and finish the flower following the methods described on pages 39 and 40–42. Here you can see the completed flower while opposite is a whole collection of different styles.

Candlestick

This project should be of particular interest to woodturners. It makes both an attractive and functional piece. I used Brazilian mahogany although its decorative grain would make walnut a superb choice. As an alternative design option, you could centre bore the stick to accept a cable and use the design as a table lamp. In addition to the waterleaf decoration (see page 50) you will use the berry moulding skills covered on page 48. You will also use a form of decoration known as gadrooning (sometimes referred to as lobing, knurling or nulling) which became popular on furniture during the early 1600s.

You can prepare the candlestick blanks by photocopying or redrawing Figs. 19 and 20 on pages 111–12 to scale. Turn your piece of timber on a lathe to the recommended size, bearing in mind that the circumferences must be the same as those in the plan drawing. Then mark one straight line running through all the sections to be carved, dividing the candlestick exactly in half. This is known as a line of symmetry (see Marking out Turnings, page 38). If you have centre bored the candlestick to accommodate electric cables, temporarily plug the holes with a dowel or cork, which will allow you to fix the nails for marking purposes.

MARKING OUT

Top Waterleaves

Set the dividers to 10mm (3/8in) and use them to gauge upwards from the bottom ridge of the section to be carved, forming a series of marks around the circumference. Then link the marks with a pencil to form a horizontal line. Now set the dividers to approximately 16mm (5/8in) and mark nine equal divisions around the horizontal line. Start from the symmetry line and finish exactly where you left off. Next realign the string (see page 39) for each dividing mark to aid drawing vertical lines down the entire length of the top section. Using the same method, divide the nine divisions above the horizontal line, forming 18 equal divisions above and nine below.

Berry Moulding

Set in a circle formed by the curved cutting edge of chisel No. 2 on a scrap piece of timber. Then set the dividers to the diameter of the circle, which should be approximately 6mm (1/4in).

Use the dividers to mark equal divisions where the berries are to be carved, taking care to do this at the base of the area rather than on the top of the ridge, otherwise you will end up with inaccurate spacing. Start and finish at the symmetry line. You may need to re-adjust your dividers several times before getting this stage right and to use the string to ensure accuracy when marking the divisions in full.

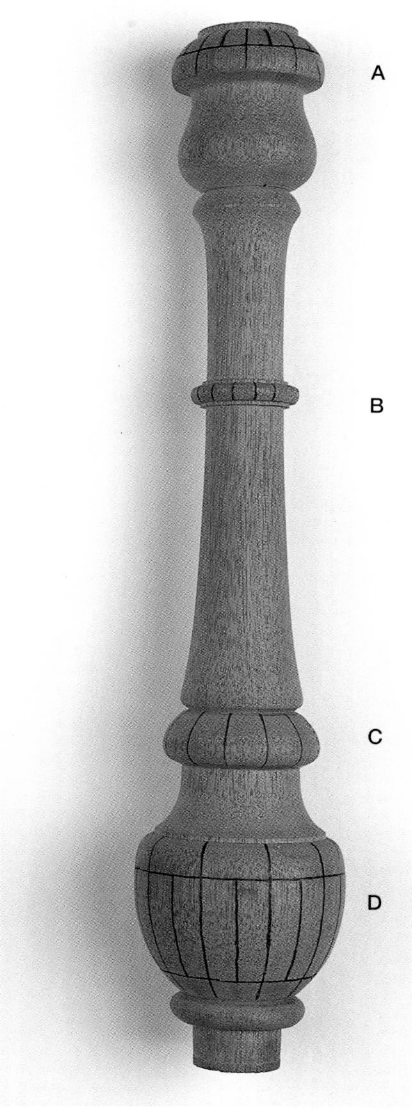

A. Top waterleaves
B. Berry moulding
C. Gadrooning
D. Bottom waterleaves

Gadrooning

Set the dividers to approximately 13mm (½in) and mark the largest circumference of the area to be carved. Complete the marking using the string to form vertical lines.

Bottom Waterleaves

Set the dividers to 13mm (½in) and measure downwards from the ridge where the leaf tips will meet the shoulder. Make a series of marks around the circumference and then link the marks with a pencil to form the upper horizontal line. Reset the dividers to 11mm (7⁄16in) and repeat this process for the bottom horizontal. Measure up from the bottom valley formed between the area to be carved and the turned ring. Next, set the dividers to a measurement of 21mm (13⁄16in) and walk them around the circumference of the top horizontal line, forming approximately 10 equal segments. Once again, start and finish in exactly the same position on the symmetry line. You may need to adjust the dividers slightly before using the string to help form perfectly straight vertical lines. Divide the segments exactly in half between the top and bottom horizontals, forming 20 even sections between the horizontals and leaving 10 above and below.

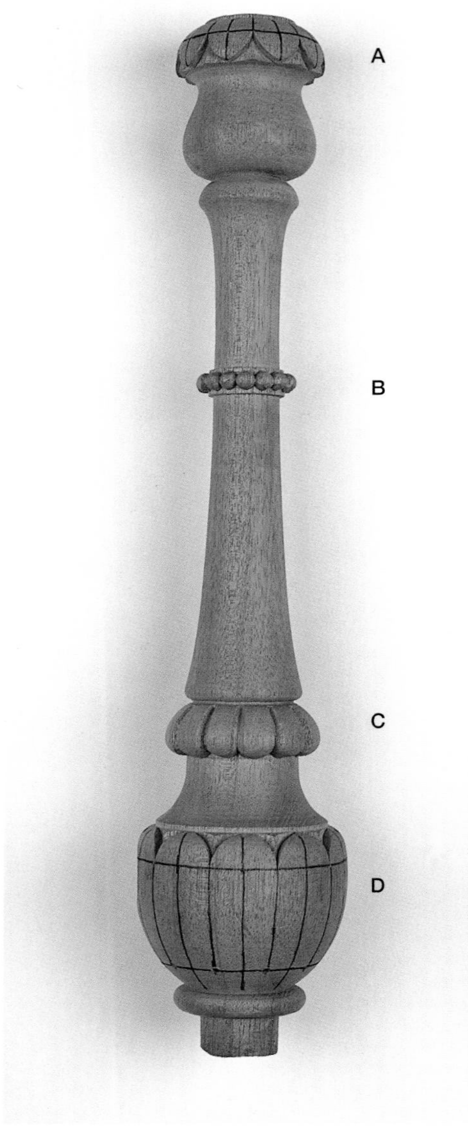

A. Top waterleaves
B. Berry moulding
C. Gadrooning
D. Bottom waterleaves

CARVING: STAGE 1

Top Waterleaves

Select chisel No. 4 and gently set in the natural curve of the cutting edge from the bottom of the nine division lines to the bottom of the 18 division lines, stopping at the horizontal mark.

Berry Moulding

Carve the division lines away with chisel No. 5, ensuring that the bottom of the valley is in the exact same position as the pencil mark.

Gadrooning

Carve a series of V lines in place of the pencil lines using chisel No. 5. Once again, ensure that the bottom of the V is located in exactly the same position as the pencil line.

Bottom Waterleaves

Set in the leaf tips with chisel No. 4 starting at the top of the smaller division line where it joins the upper horizontal to the top of the longer division line. At this stage it is only necessary to mark the timber. Next form a series of tiny drill holes on the bottom horizontal where it meets the smaller division lines. These should be approximately 3mm (⅛in) in diameter and at a depth of around 5mm (³⁄₁₆in).

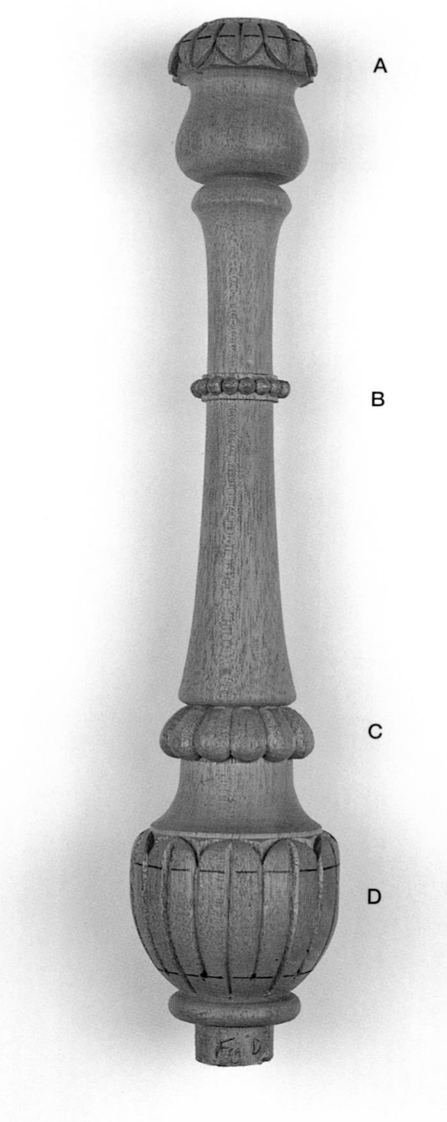

A. Top waterleaves
B. Berry moulding
C. Gadrooning
D. Bottom waterleaves

CARVING: STAGE 2

Top Waterleaves

Use chisel No. 4 to slice downwards from a halfway point between the leaf tips towards the leaf profiles which have previously been set in. The aim is to create a high central ridge which runs in line with the smaller division lines above. This series of cuts should be carefully repeated around the entire circumference.

Berry Moulding

Set in the cutting edge of chisel No. 2 along the top and bottom of each division, making the berries prominent.

Gadrooning

Gently push the cutting edge of chisel No. 3 into the end of each segment to produce a rounded shape.

Bottom Waterleaves

With chisel No. 4, form a high ridge line between the tips of the larger leaves. The ridge should run in a direct line with the smaller vertical division lines and should be formed using the same process as required for the top leaves.

Remember to slide the chisel blade towards the set in profile of each leaf, using the full length of the blade to make a clean cut. You may find it necessary to set the profile of the leaves in a little deeper so that you can more easily remove the waste timber from each of the segments.

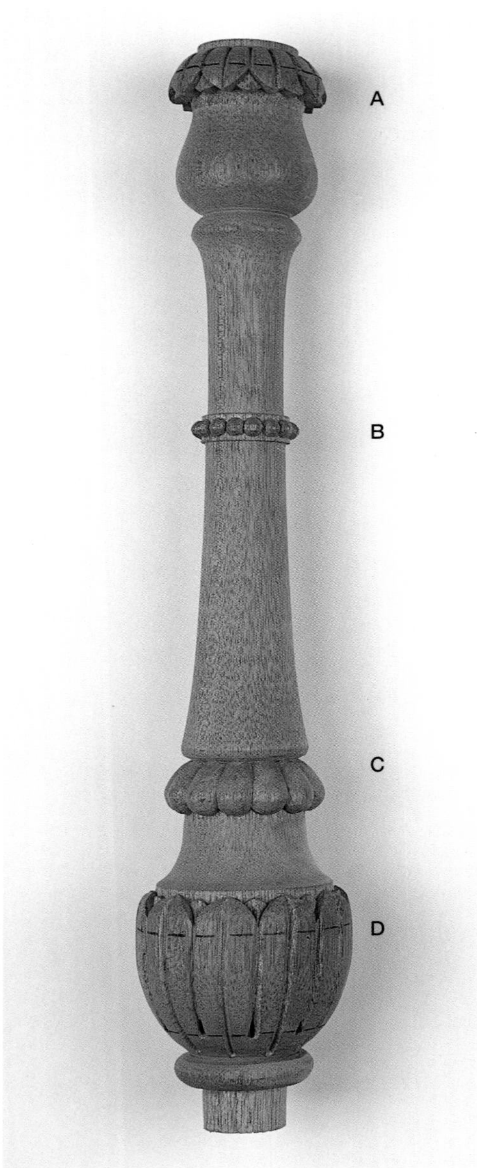

A. Top waterleaves
B. Berry moulding
C. Gadrooning
D. Bottom waterleaves

CARVING: STAGE 3

Top Waterleaves

Gently carve a V shape in place of all vertical lines with chisel No. 5. Once again, it is essential that the bottom of the valley you have created is in the precise location of the pencil line. The tapping technique is useful here.

Berry Moulding

Remove any waste fragments from between the berries using the pointed tip of chisel No. 1.

Gadrooning

Chisel No. 4 is useful to carve away the waste wood from between the lobes at their base where they join the candlestick.

Bottom Waterleaves

Use chisel No. 5 to create a valley in place of all vertical lines. Remember, accuracy is essential and take extra care as you approach the drill holes to avoid cutting past them.

If you find that you are marking the timber surrounding the holes with the sides of chisel No. 5, stop your cut just before you reach the hole. The valley can then be completed by making two cuts with chisel No. 1. Carve down towards the valley from either side, using the point of the chisel to connect with the hole.

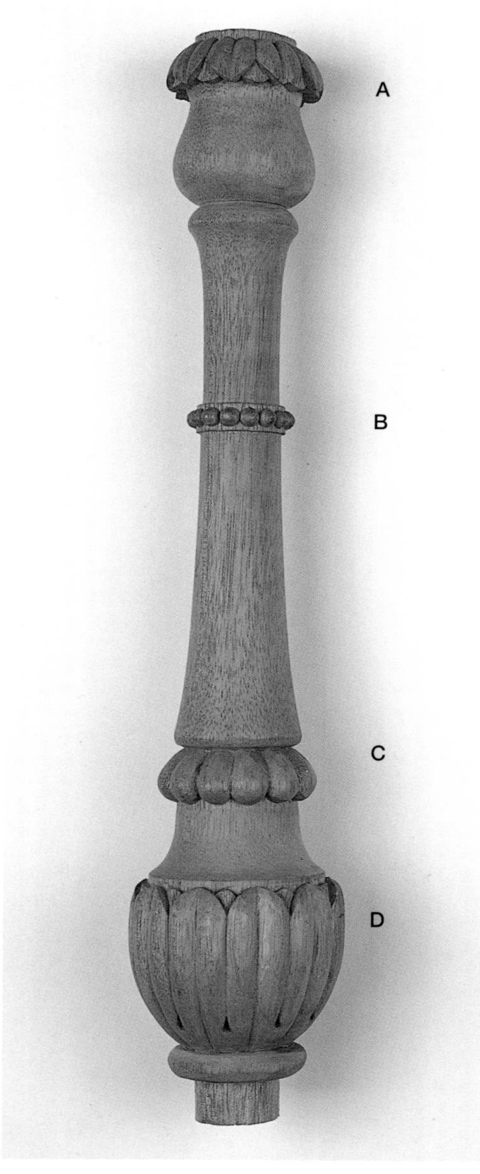

A. Top waterleaves
B. Berry moulding
C. Gadrooning
D. Bottom waterleaves

CARVING: STAGE 4

Top Waterleaves

Chisel No. 4 is ideal for creating the smaller leaves between the larger. After gently setting in their profiles you will find that chisel No. 3 is a handy size to clean away the surplus timber underneath the leaves and around the bulb.

Round the surface of the leaves into the valleys using chisel No. 4. Try to slide the chisels wherever possible as this will maximize their cutting efficiency, and then with chisel No. 1 remove the waste from around the tops of the leaves.

Berry Moulding

Hold chisel No. 2 in the fist position and round the berries over. Refer to the techniques used in the berry moulding project and try to use both hands (see page 14).

Gadrooning

With chisel No. 4, round over the surface of each of the segments. Use chisel No. 1 to remove the waste fragments from the decoration's uppermost rim. This chisel is also particularly useful for rounding over where awkward grain is encountered.

Bottom Waterleaves

Form the smaller leaves between the tips of the larger ones using chisel No. 4. Set in the profiles, forming a point for each end and remove the waste with chisel No. 1. Use chisel No. 1 to elongate the drill holes into teardrop shapes which point upwards into the valleys. Use shaped punches to help define the teardrop shape further (see page 25).

As above, round over the surface of the leaves into the valleys using chisel No. 4. Chisel No. 1 can be used once again to slice free the surplus timber.

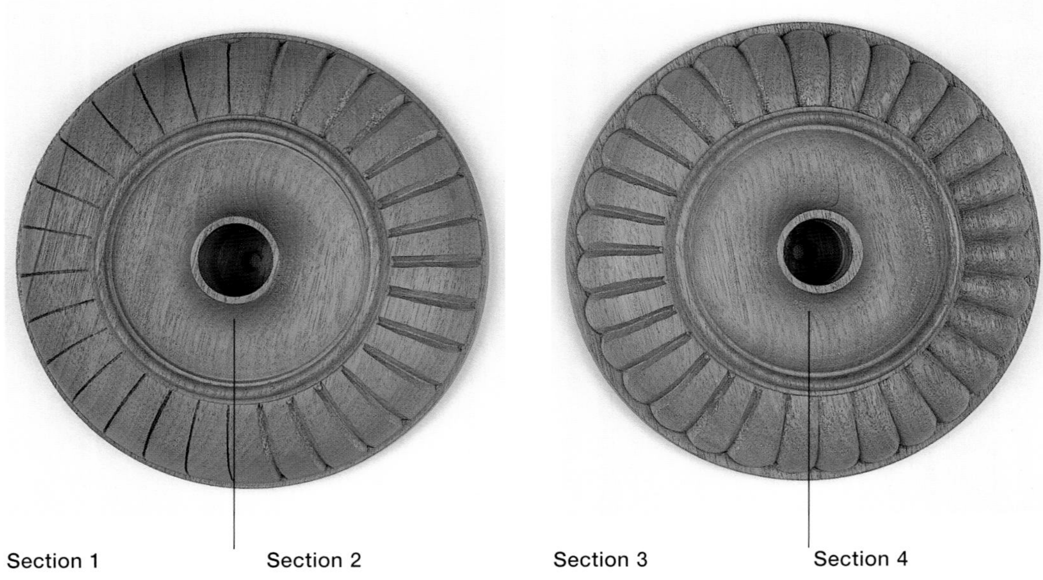

THE BASE

Section 1 After initially making a plug which sits in the candlebase hole, providing a plug for the screw to wind into, secure the base firmly to the bench using a bench screw. Then fix a nail with string attached in the centre of the plug to help you mark accurate and evenly spaced radii. Set the dividers to 20mm (¾in) and walk the points around the turning's bottom shoulder where it meets the area to be carved. You may need to re-adjust the dividers slightly to ensure that the points finish in the same position as they began. After ensuring that all divisions are exactly equal, use the string to help convert the divisions into straight lines which radiate from the centre.

Section 2 Use chisel No. 5 to replace each pencil line with a valley, taking particular care not to mark the top and bottom shoulders with the chisel. The fist position and tapping technique are both necessary for this procedure. If the valleys need to be straightened slightly, use the valley tool (see page 27).

Section 3 Set in the curve of chisel No. 4 along the front edge of each lobe where it meets the bottom shoulder to produce a rounded shape. Use chisel No. 1 to clean away any shavings that are still attached.

Section 4 Round over the square edges of each lobe into the valleys using chisel No. 4. Chisel No. 3 may also be of use to help round the lobes where they become thinner near the top shoulder. The waste timber still attached to each of the shoulders can then be trimmed away with chisel No. 1. To perfect the appearance of each section, a gentle sanding may be necessary to remove the tiny marks left by the chisel blade which only become exaggerated when polished.

Linenfold Panel

This popular panel decoration, usually found carved into oak, is thought to be of Flemish origin. The design, which symbolises ornately arranged linen, spread with local variations throughout France and Germany until it reached England towards the end of the Tudor Gothic period, around 1580. Examples can also be found on American Colonial furnishing from the seventeenth century onwards. The design is nearly always used as a panel decoration with the fold lines falling vertically.

It is believed that the design developed from the way the timber was prepared into boards. Oak in those days was sometimes 'riven', which means that the timber was planked by driving a wedge into the endgrain to force it apart. The method was much quicker than sawing and also meant that the timber tended to be stronger as the boards separated along their natural weak spots. The only problem, however, as you will realise if you have ever separated timber in this way, is that you are left with a ridged and uneven surface and it is this surface which is thought to have been adapted into what we know as the linenfold decoration.

1 Photocopy or redraw Fig. 21 on page 113 to scale and make a template. Then mark the linenfold design on to your prepared timber which should be around 20mm (3/4in) thick. Although oak is the natural choice, ash, chestnut or elm are suitable options.

Proceed to remove wood from the top and bottom areas of the design to a depth of approximately 6mm (1/4in). The reduced sections form the background, representing the surface that the linen is draped across. A router can be used to facilitate this removal.

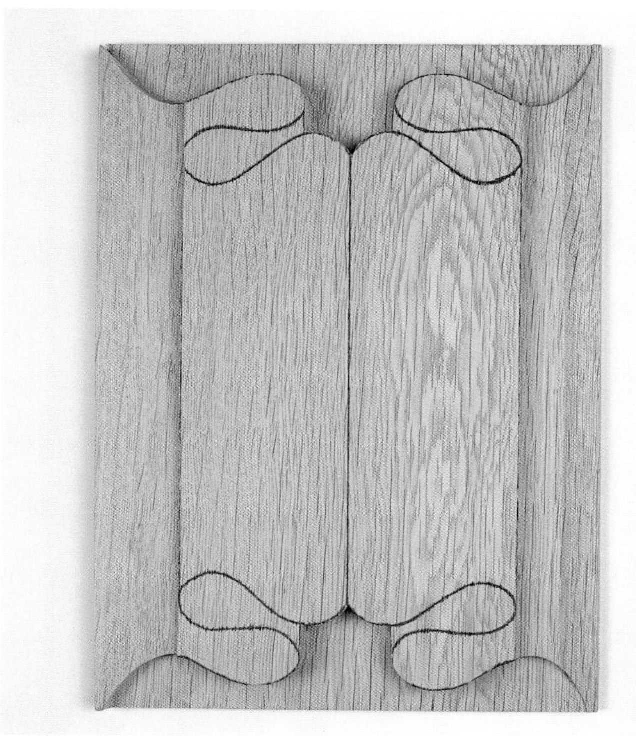

2 Use chisel No. 5 to create a V-shaped groove down the vertical lines on either side of the panel. Cut to the outside of the line in each case and then remove the waste wood with chisel No. 4 to around half the original thickness as shown on the left-hand side of the photograph. Now use chisel No. 4 to create a concave sweep forming a vertical line halfway across the section. Carve to the outside of this line, working down to the same level as the background and forming a ridge line. This creates an edge of 6mm (¼in) thickness which can be fitted into the rebate of a surrounding framework. The result can be seen on the right-hand side of the photograph.

3 Set in vertical cuts with chisel Nos. 4 and 1 to define the four loops which form the first fold on either side. Remove the waste wood by slicing towards your cut line, setting the profile in deeper as you proceed as shown left. Try to create a gentle wave-like appearance which will require deeper cuts in the centre of each of the loops.

Round over the outside edge of the first fold on each side as shown right. Chisel No. 4 will help to create the desired impression that the linen is a continuous length as it flows up into the second fold. Remember that the top and bottom of the panel must correspond.

4 Now set in the profile of the second fold on either side removing the waste wood as before with chisel Nos. 1 and 4. Then round over the outside edge of the fold with chisel No. 4, following the line established by the first fold.

Next create a ridge along the centre line of the panel by forming a long trough with chisel Nos. 3 and 4 as illustrated on the right of the photograph. Carve the surface of each fold down into the channels just created, again using chisel Nos. 4 and 1. Finally, undercut the peripheral edge of each fold to enhance the design. Remember that the aim is to create the illusion of thin material. The carving can now be sanded using sanding blocks as described on page 29.

Design Variations

After gaining an understanding of the principles of the linenfold decoration, why not try your hand at the other designs shown on pages 128–9? These feature more elaborate patterns of folds.

Fig. 34 is particularly challenging as it displays two separate pieces of linen, one draped over the other. The effect of folded material can also be incorporated into other designs. Religious carvings often depict folded parchment scriptures while heraldic carvings display ornately furled flags. Ideas can be found in books or paintings which can be used as the basis for your own designs. To make your carvings more interesting, you could decorate the folds with, for example, a band of patinated holes along the top and bottom, or following the line of each fold to provide an edge detail.

Tudor Rose

The Tudor rose is a decoration steeped in tradition and history. The rose has long held a symbolic place in decorative art in many countries, cultures and religions. Used to depict innocence, knowledge, peace and suffering as well as love, passion, secrecy and sacrifice, it is hardly surprising that this symbol of so many values became such a common heraldic motif and was, and still is, incorporated into furniture designs and used widely in archictecture.

Briefly, the story of the Tudor rose dates back to 1455 when civil war broke out in England between the Lancastrians and the Yorkists, both sides fighting for the throne and political power. The Lancastrians carried the badge of a red rose while the Yorkists fought under the emblem of the white rose. In 1485, Henry Tudor, the Lancastrians' leader, took the throne, crowning himself Henry VII. On his marriage to Elizabeth of York he combined the red and white rose badges, creating what became known as the Tudor rose and marking the official end of the War of the Roses.

Not surprisingly, this design became an important decoration on wood and stonework throughout the Tudor period (1485–1603) and beyond. It was also frequently used on embroidered tapestries and in paintwork.

1 Using Fig. 22 on page 114, make a stencil by first cutting a card circle with a diameter of approximately 200mm (8in). Divide the circle using a protractor into five equal sections formed by radial lines, each with an angle of 72°. Cut a series of slots along these divisions, not quite to the outside edge, allowing a pencil to mark the timber beneath. (If you are carving a number of roses you could make a complete stencil.) Then mark the design on to your prepared timber. The Tudor rose is traditionally carved into oak but hardwoods such as ash, elm or chestnut would be suitable alternatives. It is traditional to have one petal at the top and two at the bottom.

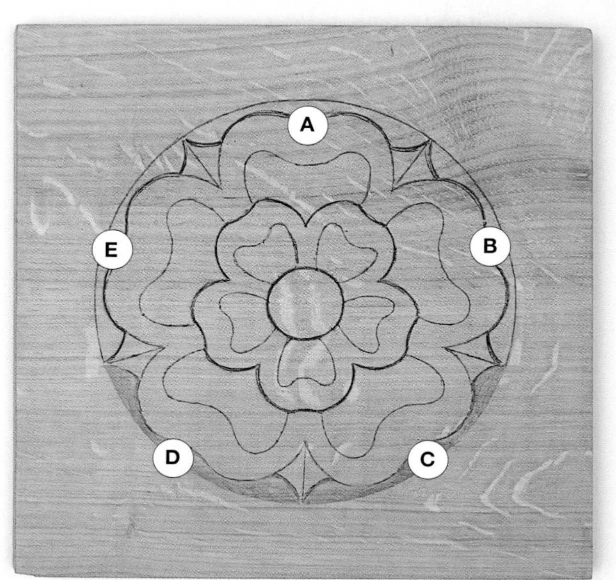

2 Set in the outside profile of the large rose, small rose and inner circle with vertical cuts from chisel No. 4 as shown on petals A, B and E. Then use chisel No. 4 to carve from the surrounding circle towards the set in cut to define the larger rose. This stage can be seen between petals C and D. Do not carve outside the circle.

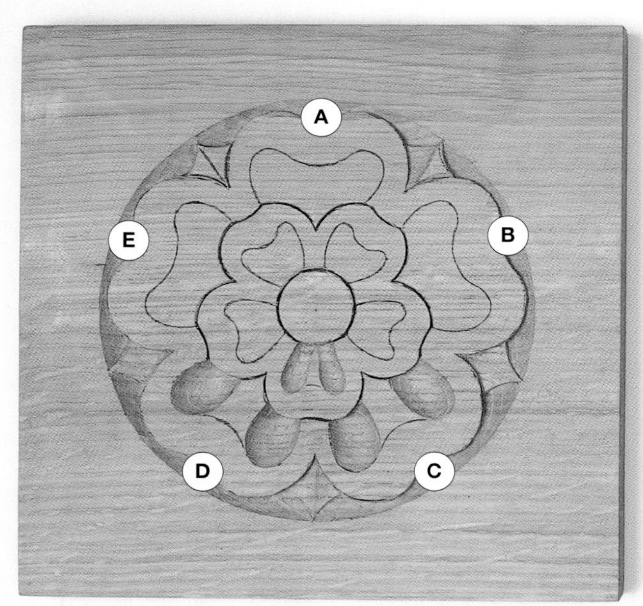

3 Here you can see that the shape of the left-hand barb on petal A has been set in with chisel No. 4. The right-hand barb has been developed further by carving downwards from the centre line to the set in cut. Now carve downwards in the opposite direction from the central line, leaving a high ridge in the middle, as shown between petals B and C.

Concentrate now on shaping the large rose petals, using chisel No. 3 to cut two channels as shown for C and D. These should be within the confines of the internally marked lines, leaving a high area in the centre of each petal. Create the same effect for each petal of the smaller rose, this time using chisel No. 2.

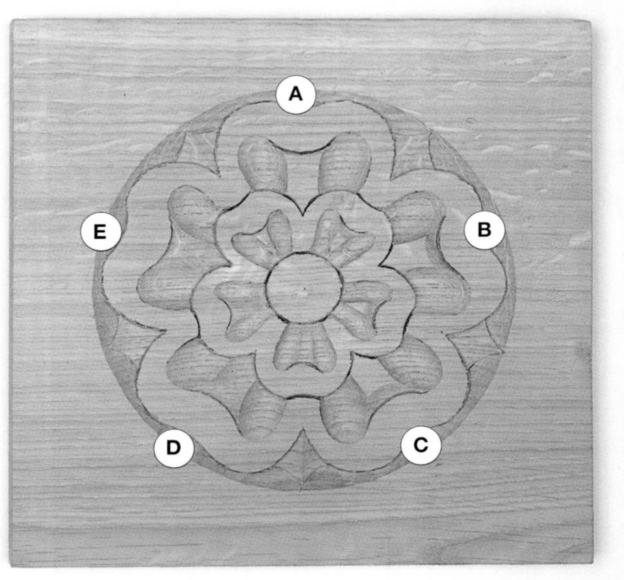

4 Set in the inner curved line of each of the large petals with chisel No. 4 as shown on petal A. Next remove a slice by angling a cut towards the previous one, again with chisel No. 4. Continue this effect, as illustrated on petals B and C, around all the larger petals. Use the same series of cuts on the smaller rose, this time using chisel No. 3 to set in the internal curve and produce the angled slice.

Now use chisel No. 3 to carve a channel in the centre of the large petals, forming two clean flowing ridges on either side. This is illustrated on petals D and E. On the smaller petal next to D, the same series of cuts has been made, this time using chisel No. 2.

5 Carve the area where petals A and B meet down towards the smaller rose using chisel No. 1. Repeat this process for all of the larger petals and for the smaller rose where it meets the central circle. With chisel No. 5, carve a V-shaped line to divide the petals as shown where petals C and D meet. The line should be aimed directly towards the centre of the design. Chisel No. 1 may also be used in areas of awkward grain by setting in the line and slicing down towards it on either side.

To complete the seeds in the centre, first cut an inner circle with chisel No. 2. Then mark eight equal divisions radiating from the centre of the circle and with chisel No. 2 cut an arc at the widest point of each division forming a continuous link of cuts. Complete the seeds by setting in each division line with chisel No. 1 and slice down towards it from either side to form a valley. Round over each berry with chisel No. 2 and remove the waste with chisel No. 1. Use chisel No. 1 to complete each petal by rounding over and smoothing the outside edges. Finally, sand the work gently.

Acanthus Panel

This project provides an introduction to the most commonly used and tradtional form of leaf decoration. It creates a very attractive panel which can be incorporated into chair backs, coffer sides, cupboard doors and jewellery box lids. It even makes a stylish wall decoration in its own right. The acanthus leaf decoration here is fairly simple, but once you are confident that you understand the principles of the leaf design (see pages 34–6) it can be made more elaborate and used to decorate almost any area whether flat or turned.

1 Photocopy or redraw Fig. 22 on page 114 to scale (you may find it helpful to refer also to the section on drawing acanthus leaves on pages 34–6). Notice that all lines defining the outer edges of the leaves radiate in gentle sweeps towards the centre berry. Mark the design, including internal lines, on to the timber (African mahogany here). If you intend to carve a repetitive pattern it would be sensible to make a stencil from stiff card as shown above.

2 With chisel No. 5, set in a V line around the diamond shape which surrounds the acanthus leaves. Anchor the chisel firmly to avoid unwanted slips. Use the valley tool to neaten the cut if necessary. Set in the outline of the acanthus design and the centre berry using chisel Nos. 2, 3 and 4. At this stage it is only necessary to mark the surface of the timber.

3 Define the leaf design from the surrounding timber, creating the illusion that the motif is placed on top of precut chamfers. Using chisel No. 1, carefully slice down to the lines you have previously set in. Deepen the cuts progressively as you work, ensuring that the surface line of the chamfer is perfectly straight.

Now form four eyelets, giving the impression that parts of leaves overlap others. This helps to provide a sense of depth and a three-dimensional appearance. With chisel No. 3 make a cut leading to where each eye hole is to be located. Cut towards it and remove a small segment of wood with chisel No. 2. The shape can be defined further using a shaped punch (see page 25).

4 Use chisel No. 2 to set in the four circles located in the diagonal border. Round over the wood inside to form a berry (see berry moulding project, page 48), trying not to damage the outside surface. Now slice down towards the larger oval-shaped berry in the centre of the leaf design with chisel Nos. 3 and 4. Deepen the groove surrounding the berry to a depth of 5–7mm (3⁄16–9⁄32in) and remove the waste.

5 Round over the centre berry with chisel Nos. 3 and 4. Make sure you anchor the chisel and use the tapping technique. Next use chisel No. 3 to scoop out the shape of the leaves between each line, working inwards. Carve shallowly where the lines are close together and deeper where they are further apart. The original pencil lines should remain visible, forming ridges or high points which flow towards the centre. Remember to slide the chisels.

Divide the remaining flat sections with pencil lines, ensuring these, too, flow towards the centre berry. As before, scoop out the wood between the lines with chisel No. 2, creating another set of ridges which flow towards the centre. Finally, gently sand the finished decoration being careful not to round over any details.

Lettering

The art of lettering is a tremendously popular form of carving because of its infinite applications. Names carved in wood can make treasured gifts or house signs while poems and favourite catch phrases can be documented in a way that will survive the centuries. You may wish to initial or date pieces of your work, incorporating personal details into your very own logo.

After marking out and accurately spacing your letters, the carving is actually quite simple. However, as with all projects, the carving is a direct representation of the drawing. Therefore, a great deal of importance must be placed on marking out the letters correctly before starting to carve.

STYLE

There are many styles of lettering to choose from, some plain, some fancy and many in between. It is important to make sure that the style suits the application. For a house sign which needs to be clear for people driving by, for instance, a plain style would be appropriate. Another point to consider is whether individual letters are recognisable. Initially, this may seem a strange consideration, but it is an extremely valid one for certain styles. For example, the letter illustrated in Fig. 24 on page 116 is an old English letter J. It could be mistaken for a T or I. Therefore, this style of lettering could potentially lead to confusion when used for initials before a surname.

SPACING AND DEFINITION

A common problem is encountered by carvers who break down words into the number of letters and then mark out equally proportioned boxes for each. The result when the letters are positioned is, of course, irregular and non-flowing. This is because few letters are of exactly the same proportions. Take, for example, the letters I and M. The solution is to draw them freehand and space them to appear visually correct as opposed to mathematically correct. The height of letters is a slightly different matter. A standard height for upper and lower case letters should be established and maintained throughout the sign. This can be regulated by drawing three parallel lines on to the timber. A common scale is that lower case letters are one third smaller than upper.

Inevitably aesthetics play the key role. Ensure spacing between words is equal and that the distance between word lines is sufficient to avoid overcrowding (see picture opposite).

It is possible to give prominence to certain words by carving them larger than others.

REGULATING LETTER FORM

Study the example styles provided on pages 117–118. Note that each letter is drawn with a variation of thin lines, developing into thick. Transfer these to your carving to add interest, and regulate the thicknesses throughout the text. For example, set the thin lines at 2mm ($\frac{1}{16}$in) and the thick lines at 5mm ($\frac{3}{16}$in) and adhere to these guidelines from start to finish.

ANGLE OF LETTERS

Attention should be given to the angle of the letters. If they are drawn with a slight slant, then efforts are necessary to maintain this angle.

POSITION OF WORDS

When marking out words remember to consider their position in relation to the borders of the sign itself. What you do not want is beautifully spaced letters forming words which are all located slightly off centre.

FINISHING

Make sure, when completing the marking out, that the lines of each letter are clean and crisp, with clearly defined edges. Remember drawing is the first stage of carving. If the drawing is unclear then the carving is almost guaranteed to be the same.

REFERENCE

It is useful to build up collections of different styles of lettering. Letter transfers are ideal. Take photographs of interesting signs in the street and study the layout and proportions.

INCISED LETTERS

Incised letter carving is a relatively quick and easy method which is, therefore, ideal for the beginner to tackle first. The four styles of letters illustrated in Figs. 25 and 26 (pages 117 and 118) vary in difficulty due to the combination of straight and curved lines. At the top and bottom of each line on three of the styles you will probably notice an additional cut forming a 'flick'. These flicks are known as serifs. Concentrate primarily on an easy style as illustrated in Fig. 25 and carve a letter formed by straight lines only, such as the letter A as shown on page 86.

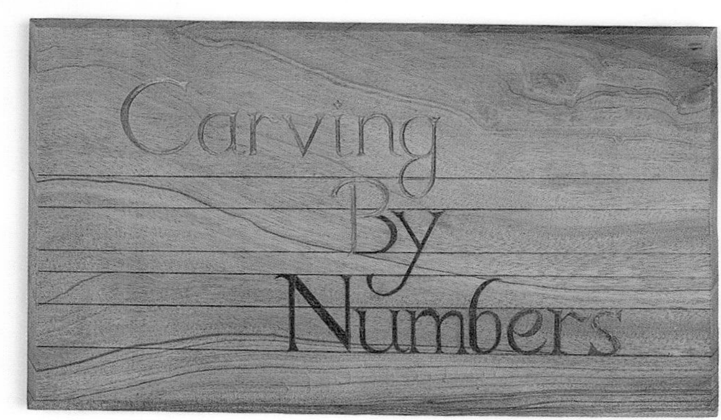

An example of incised lettering.

RELIEF LETTERS

The instruction provided on page 87 will give you a firm understanding of the principles and techniques required to carve relief lettering. To demonstrate these I have chosen the old English style. This is considered a challenging font as each letter is decorated with fine details from which the background must be reduced. When carving any style of letter in relief, a 13mm (½in) flat bevel-edged chisel is a useful addition to your toolkit. For first attempts it may be wise to choose a plainer style of letter.

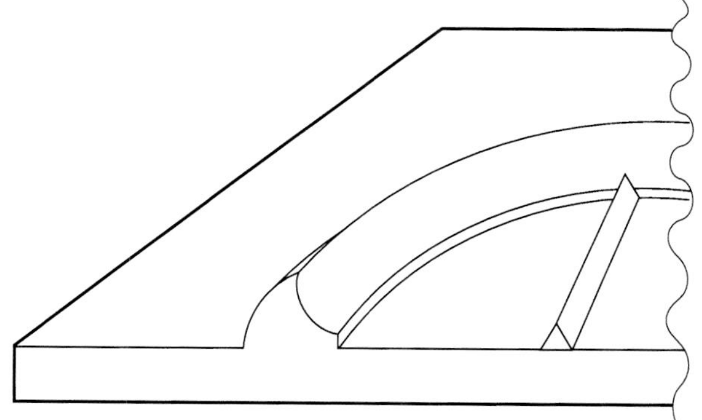

Fig. 10

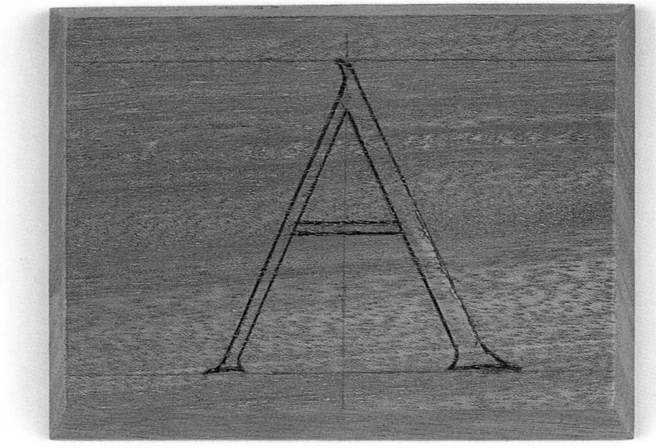

1 Mark the letter out, referring to the previous suggestions. Using chisel No. 1 or a 13mm (½in) flat bevel-edged chisel, make the first incision. The edges of the letter must be angled towards each other at around 45° to form a V cross section.

A clean, straight line should be formed as the walls meet. Ensure that the lower valley line is central to the upper lines. You can begin the valleys using chisel No. 5, but finish with chisel No. 1 or a flat chisel in order to maintain clean, straight surface lines.

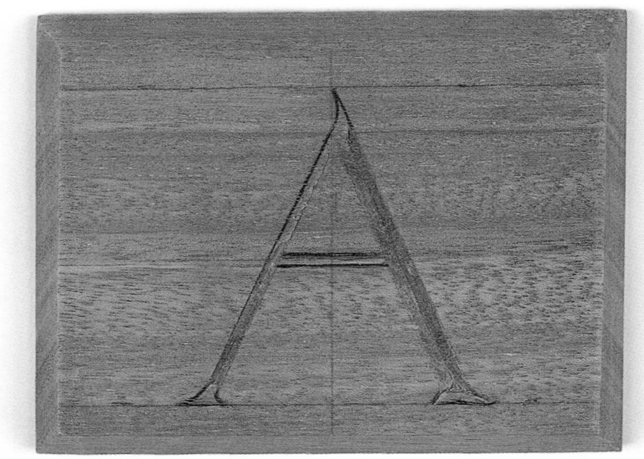

2 Notice here how the letter is developing. The thinner line of the A has been partly formed. The depth of cut should be less for thinner lines.

Use chisel No. 1 to create an inverted pyramid effect for the serifs at the point where all the edges meet.

3 Use fine sandpaper wrapped around a sanding block to remove any pencil marks apparent on the timber's surface, and clean up any wandering lines with chisel No. 1.

To develop your skills further try carving a letter that incorporates curves. The letter R is an ideal choice. Note in Fig. 26 how the curve varies in thickness from wide to narrow. This should be duplicated, remembering that the line where the walls of the letter meet should constantly remain central to the surface lines. The real test is to carve the letter S. Form the curved lines using chisel Nos. 2, 3 and 4.

1 Mark out the profile of the letter on to the surface of the timber. It may help to shade the letter totally to make the whole shape visibly clearer as shown here. The next stage is to remove the background, a process for which a router may come in handy.

2 Remove the background to distinguish the letter. Ensure that the letter walls are at 90° to the reduced area so that the edges do not change shape as they are carved lower.

Just as with incised letters the valley depth varied according to the width of the lines, the same principle also applies in relief, forming an opposite impression. Instead of a valley line, create a ridge line. The ridge will be lower as the line becomes thinner as illustrated in Fig. 10. Ensure the ridge line is central to its outer edges. If the line is curved, carve a concave profile on the concave side and vice versa.

3 The finished letter is shown here. Note how extra depth can be added to your carving by allowing certain components to overlap others. An example of this is evident halfway around the crescent shaped section.

The background has been stamped to define the letter further with a punch (see page 25).

Flowers and Leaves

This attractive carving will encourage you to start thinking in three dimensions. Inspired by a Victorian design it is not elaborately detailed but provides scope for shaping in various ways. Once finished it can be applied to a door panel or used as an embellishment for the centre of a plinth below a cornice moulding. It can also be used as a decorative wall hanging set into a picture frame. I would suggest mahogany for this project although this choice is not essential.

Provided the formation of the leaf divisions is the same on either side, the shaping does not need to be exactly symmetrical.

1 Photocopy or redraw Fig. 27 on page 119 to scale and make a template from a piece of card. Trace around the template on to your piece of wood which should be no less than 30mm (1 ¼in) thick. Then cut out the shape using a bandsaw or coping saw, taking care to cut on the waste side of the line. It does not matter at this stage if the basic shape is very rough as it can easily be tidied up with the chisels later. The blank must be firmly secured before you begin to carve. I recommend gluing it to a board which can be cramped to your worksurface (see page 32).

2 Ensuring that the grain is pointing away from you, set in the edges of the flowers with chisel Nos. 3 and 4. The cuts must be made at 90°. Start to remove the surrounding wood with chisel No. 4, setting in the original cuts more deeply as you work. Continue until the timber around the flower heads is reduced to a thickness of around 15mm (⅝in). Aim for a flat surface around the flowers using a flat bevel edged chisel or chisel No. 1. You could alternatively use a router for this stage. Now pencil in the markings shown, dividing the design down the middle with curved lines to left and right. These curves will later become high ridges when carved.

3 With chisel No. 5, carefully carve down between the curved lines below the flower heads to form a valley. Use chisel No. 1 to cut more deeply as the ridges get further apart. Try to define the bottom of the valley with one clean straight line. Continue this method to extend the valley beneath each leaf, forming a recess which is roughly triangular in shape.

4 You can now start to shape the leaves removing small slices at a time with chisel Nos. 1, 3 and 4. Start hollowing from the sides and leave the central section higher. Carve the edges of the leaves lower, trying to achieve a fine appearance at the tips. Think about each cut you make and visualize how you want the leaf to lie. It may be useful to collect leaves from the garden for reference. Next form the scrolls by setting in each shape with chisel No. 3 and removing the excess timber from around the cuts with chisel Nos. 3 and 4.

5 Once you have shaped the leaves satisfactorily, you can round over the scrolls with chisel No. 4. Hold the chisel in the fist position and gently round the edges over, sliding the cutting edge as you work to make it more effective. At this point pencil in the leaf divisions, the circle in the centre of each flower and the petals as shown. Ensure that the divisions flow towards the central line for each leaf. Next set in the circle in the centre of each flower with chisel No. 3 and, using chisel Nos. 3 and 4, divide the petals evenly, carving each as if it is slightly overlapping the next.

6 Now start to carve in between the lines marked on the acanthus leaves with chisel No. 3, replacing the lines with a series of ridges which flow towards the leaf divisions. Work carefully as you may encounter awkward grain at this stage. Once you have formed the first set of ridges, you can pencil in a second set of lines, carving between them with chisel No. 2. This process creates another set of flowing ridge lines to give added interest and a sense of movement to the leaves. Using chisel No. 1, divide the valley just below the flower heads and between the leaves once again on either side to form two small triangular-shaped sections. This will create the impression of stems being atttached to the flowers.

Finally, gently remove the work from the board with a pallet knife following the instructions on page 32. Just to give the carving an extra touch, you can back off the leaves (see page 39). Gently slice the wood from underneath the edges of the leaves at a slight angle so that when you look at the carving straight on the thickness is hidden.

Swag

Swags comprise elongated amalgams of decorative motifs which are usually interwoven amongst leaf work. The arrangements are carved as though they are draped or hanging and are used for interior and architectural decoration. Grinling Gibbons (1648–1726), who was famed for his incredibly ornate work, produced some outstanding examples featuring fruit, leafwork, flowers, birds, musical instruments and cherubs.

The versatile aspect of this decoration is that you can make it as simple or complicated as you wish. Fig. 28 shows a relatively simple design but you may feel confident about adding greater detail perhaps to the flower as shown in the photographs. It is very important to follow the stages of woodcarving as outlined on page 38 for this project.

1 Make a stencil using Fig. 28 on page 120. Then mark the drawing on to your piece of timber which should be around 45mm (1 ¾in) thick. I used a piece of old pine which was extremely well seasoned, but you may find a good quality Brazilian mahogany rather more attractive if the carving is to be polished. Lime is an outstanding timber for intricately detailed carvings. (It is probably for this reason that it was used by Grinling Gibbons for much of his work.) The profile of the design should now be cut out using a band, coping or fret saw and then secured to the worksurface using the method described on page 32.

Whether your decision is to follow the detailed instruction or to carve a more simplistic version, it is necessary to mark on to the carving blank the details as shown. This will provide you with the basic shape guidelines.

2 Start to carve the high and low areas of the design using each of the five chisels as appropriate. All the invidual components should be distinguishable from each other. It is wise to consider overlapping the items to avoid empty spaces on the carving where irregular shapes do not fit neatly together. Potential problem areas could be around spherical objects such as the plum and rose. Note how the flowers and plum are carved high and the leaves are reduced to provide a background

3 Having established the various heights of each component, carefully plan their shape. While it would be rather ambitious to make the leaves as thin and fine as their natural counterparts, do try to give them as much movement and character as possible. Avoid leaving them high around the edges as this will allow a view underneath, revealing their true thickness. For example note that the three acanthus leaves at the top of the design are carved with their centres high and their edges rounded downwards. If an empty space appears, try to create something from it such as the surface of a lower leaf. Pierced holes may be effective in some places though too many will look unattractive. After shaping each component, carve the edges of the acanthus leaves into their primary forms (see page 35).

4 When you have defined the overall shape of the swag, you can begin to add the detail. Work on the acanthus leaves and form the flowers. Remember that your own swag need not be as detailed as this one. Rather than carving the rose with open petals, simply form a closed bud. Silk flowers provide an excellent source of reference. Chisel Nos. 3 and 4 should be used to form the petals and chisel No. 1 to remove the waste fragments. Carve a groove down the side of the plum with chisel No. 5.

5 Now add the final details. Using chisel Nos. 2, 3 and 4 cut small channels on the surface of each leaf forming ridges which sweep down towards the base of the leaf. Each leaf and petal should be slightly undercut to produce a finer appearance. Round the plum with chisel No. 1 and form ridges with chisel No. 2 on the petals of the second flower. Each petal of the third flower could be broken down carefully into the primary acanthus form using chisel Nos. 1 and 2. Use chisel No. 2 also to create channels on the surface of each petal.

Sand the swag lightly to remove any remaining tool marks. Take care not to round over any details or crisp lines however.

Corbel

The corbel is a much used form of applied decoration most commonly found on carcase furnishing. Their design varies tremendously according to functional requirements and the tastes of different periods. You can often see them supporting the protruding mouldings and sills of impressive historical buildings. On furniture, their function is mostly ornamental and examples of some interesting variations are illustrated on page 99. The corbel shown here makes use of the acanthus leaf decoration and also incorporates flutes and scrolls.

1 Photocopy or redraw Figs. 29a and b on page 121 to scale and use them to produce stencils. For this project you will need to start off with a piece of timber 150 x 50 x 50mm (6 x 2 x 2in). Once again I used Brazilian mahogany for this project, but oak, pine, beech, rosewood and walnut are other possibilities. Mark the two best faces of the timber with the face side and face edge symbols. Then place the stencil formed by Fig. 29a on to the face side, mark around its edge and cut the profile out as accurately as possible.

2 After cutting the first profile of the corbel, place the stencil formed by Fig. 29b on the face edge, draw around it and cut out the shape. If you have access to a bandsaw, you will find this the quickest and easiest method of cutting the blank. When using a fret or coping saw, take your time to ensure that the cut is equal on both sides.

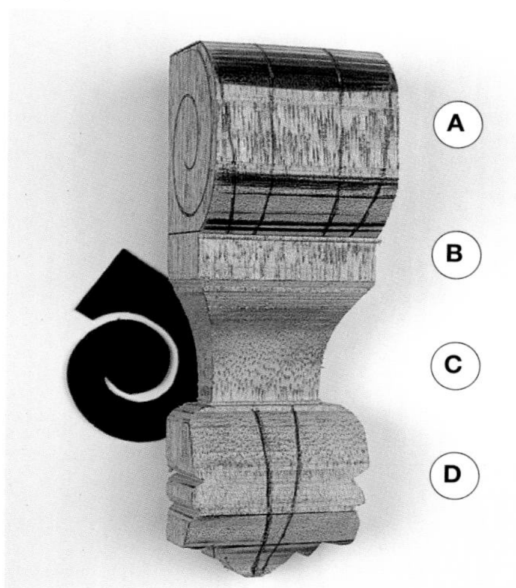

3 Mark the two central parallel lines that divide area A into three equal portions. Then divide the outer portions with diagonal lines that fall from the very top of the blank's outer edge to the middle of the division where area A meets B. Also mark the side scroll on both sides of section A using a stencil. Next form the elongated V line required on section D. At its widest point the V should be exactly 12mm (½in), narrowing to 1mm (1⁄32in) in width at the very bottom of the design. This V will form the central vein for the acanthus leaf design.

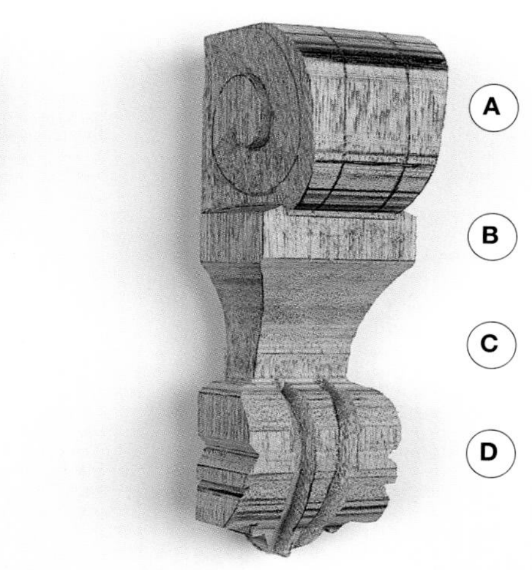

4 With chisel Nos. 3 and 4, set in the profile of the scroll on both sides of section A, making sure that the cuts are made at 90°. Then with chisel No. 1 or a 20mm (¾in) flat bevel-edged chisel, carve the outer diagonal lines of section A down to the set in cuts of the side scrolls. Notice the diagonal cut does not continue to the rear of the design, but tapers out to the full width of the corbel. Finally use chisel No. 5 to form two deep V-shaped grooves to define the central vein of the acanthus leaf on section D. Hold the chisel at a slight angle, providing the vein with vertical side walls.

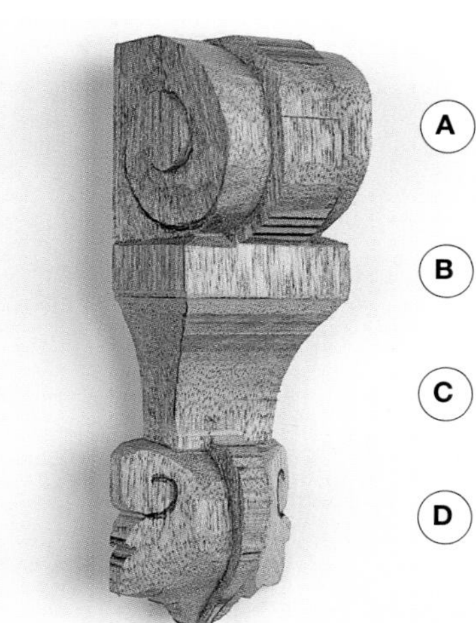

5 Define the central portion of section A using chisel No. 5, ensuring that the side walls are vertical to the surface of the wood. Then with chisel No. 1 or a flat 20mm (¾in) bevel-edged chisel, reduce the two outer portions of area A to follow the profile of the side scroll.

The next stage is to shape section D as shown. Remove most of the timber with chisel No. 4 and round over the surface with chisel No. 1, which will then allow you to mark the scrolls on either side.

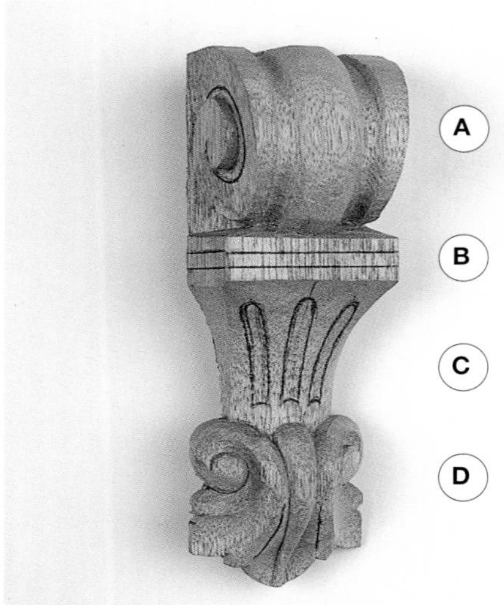

6 The lower part of section C is rounded with chisel No. 1. Set in the scrolls on section D with chisel Nos. 2 and 3 and define their shape by slicing down towards the cut lines with chisel No. 3. Now form a channel with chisel No. 3 to shape the two large side leaves of section D. This should form two high ridge lines that flow in the line of the scroll. Round over the central vein of section D, and the high central ridge of section A with chisel No. 4 and carve two deep troughs with chisel No. 2 on either side. Mark the side scrolls of section A with a spiralling line and pencil in additional markings on sections B, C and D as shown.

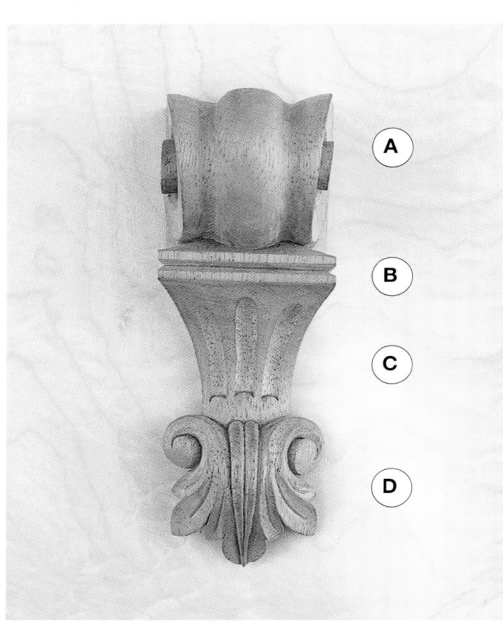

7 Develop the side scrolls of section A with chisel Nos. 3 and 4 by setting the edges lower. Then slice down at an angle from the spiralling line just marked towards the deepened perimeter cut to create a ridge line defining each scroll further. Use chisel No. 2 to form the smaller channels on the acanthus leaves on section D.

With chisel No. 5 carve a small V-shaped channel down the middle of the central vein in section D and round over each side. Now decorate the leaves further, adding individual veins by making very shallow cuts down the centre of each leaf with chisel No. 5. Draw the lines in pencil first to provide a guide. Use chisel No. 2 to set in the three semicircular bases of the flutes on section C. Then carve within the pencil lines to create the flutes themselves, again with chisel No. 2. Form a deep V-shaped channel between the lines marked along the top and sides of section B with chisel No. 5. If you encounter awkward grain, you could use chisel No. 1.

Finally, clean up the outside edges of the leaves. To complete the corbel use the technique of backing off as described on page 39. Then give the work a gentle sanding.

Decorative Bracket

This decorative bracket incorporates the techniques and designs used in several of the earlier projects. The top shelf is surrounded by a quadrant moulding decorated by waterleaves, and paterae are used on the sides of the bracket. Both these decorations are of exactly the same dimensions as those shown on pages 50 and 60. When mounted on a wall, the bracket provides a wonderful platform for an ornament. Alternatively, you could use two or more brackets to support a shelf.

This project encourages you to develop your skills and understanding of the acanthus leaf design. You will almost certainly need to refer to the section on pages 34–6 which clearly shows the development of an acanthus illustration. As with all projects, bear in mind that what you carve is a direct reflection of what you draw. It is important also to give the impression that parts of the leaf overlap, which is achieved by forming eylets. This enhances the three-dimensional appearance and finesse of the piece.

1 Photocopy or redraw Figs. 30a, b and c on pages 122 and 123 to the correct scale. You will need to make stencils for each one. Mark the outline of stencil A on to a piece of wood 200 x 120 x 95mm (8 x 4 ¾ x 3 ¾in). I used reclaimed pine, but there are many hard and softwood alternatives such as oack, mahogany and lime. Use a bandsaw to cut out the shape. Bend stencils 30a and c around the carving blank. (The illustrations take into account the increased surface area created by the curvature of the design.) Secure the bracket in a vice and set in the circles on both sides.

2 Remove a little wood from each circle with chisel No. 4, forming a flat bottom at a depth of 7mm (5⁄16in). A router may be useful for this stage. With chisel No. 5 carve a groove defining either side of the long scroll. Now use chisel No. 1 to define the small leaf shape on the side of the bracket and top curve of the circle. Develop these details with V-shaped cuts, forming an inverted pyramid. Then use chisel No. 4 to set in the rounded profile of the bottom of the scroll on each side. Scoop away the surrounding timber to meet the cut.

To develop the acanthus leaf on the front of the bracket, form the two grooves marking the centre stem using chisel No. 5. Then set in and define each section of the leaf with chisel Nos. 1, 3 and 4. Work down towards the V cuts which define each side scroll as you carve the edges of the leaf divisions.

3 Next carve the edges of the leaf on either side of the bracket down towards the border of the scroll with chisel No. 4, forming flowing ridge lines. Then carve the section of the scroll where the circle meets the long curve to make it appear that the bottom edge of the circle is passing beneath at this point. Create a slightly dished effect along the surface of the scroll's border, imagining it as a racing track. As this 'track' heads away from the circle, bank the edges using chisel No. 4. Carve a fluted shape above the bottom of the scroll with chisel No. 3. This creates two ridges, one forming the side of the track and the other producing a small ridge where the timber falls below the front leaf decoration.

Pencil in the leaf markings on the front of the bracket and shape each division using chisel Nos. 1 and 4. Carve channels on each leaf section using chisel Nos. 2 and 3. The aim is to form high ridge lines that emphasize and add interest to each division as shown on the right of the photograph (see Drawing Acanthus Leaves, page 34).

4 Complete the small leaf on either side of the bracket with chisel No. 2, forming two flutes that create a centre ridge. Thin down the front leaf, where it flicks over, to look less cumbersome. This technique is described on page 39. Add further flutes to the front acanthus leaves, ensuring all ridges formed are flowing correctly. Divide the centre stem with chisel No. 5 and round over the edges with chisel No. 1.

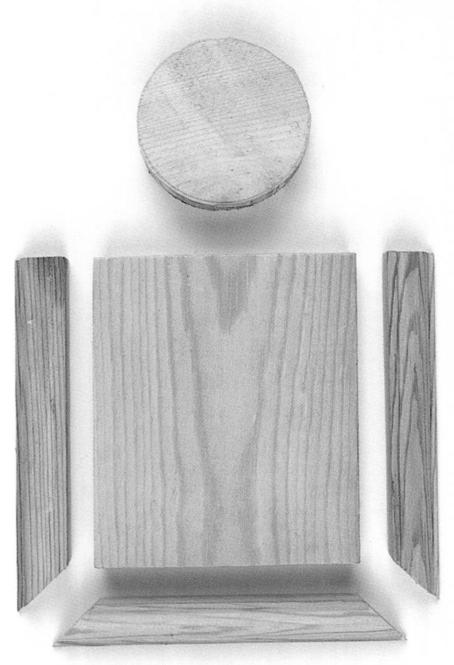

5 Next construct the top shelf from the components shown. (The circular blank is the first stage in making a patera.) On completion, secure it to the bracket with a couple of panel pins or dowels. The dimensions for the shelf before the moulding is added should be the exact size of the top surface of the bracket, approximately 120 x 95mm (4 ¾ x 3 ¾in). Decorate the shelf with a waterleaf moulding, following the instructions on page 50.

To complete the bracket, make two paterae following the steps on pages 60–62 and insert these into the circles on the sides of the bracket. Finally, give the piece a light sanding, taking care not to round over any edges.

Plan Drawings

Note

One grid square represents 20mm (25⁄32in) throughout the plan drawings section.

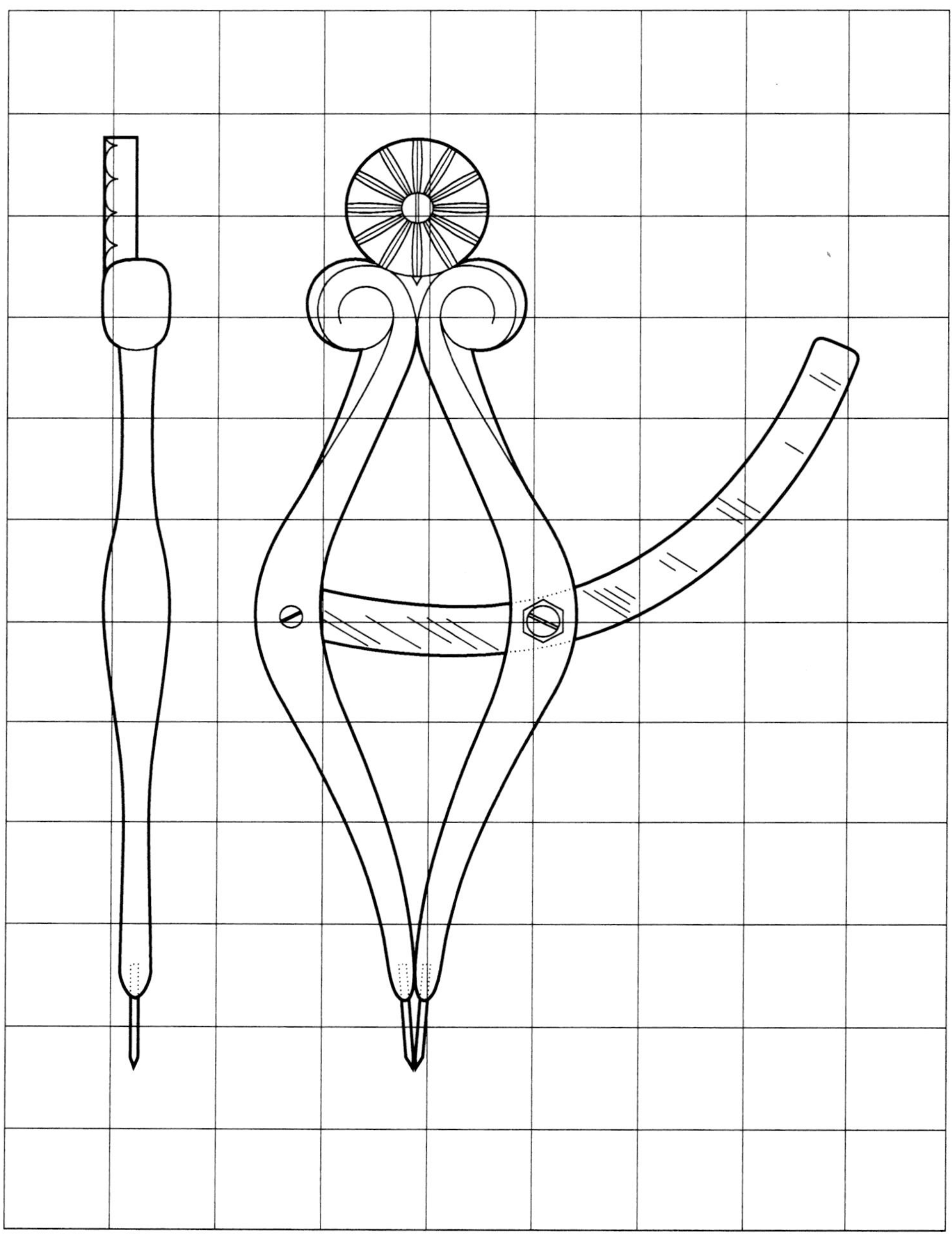

Fig. 11 Dividers

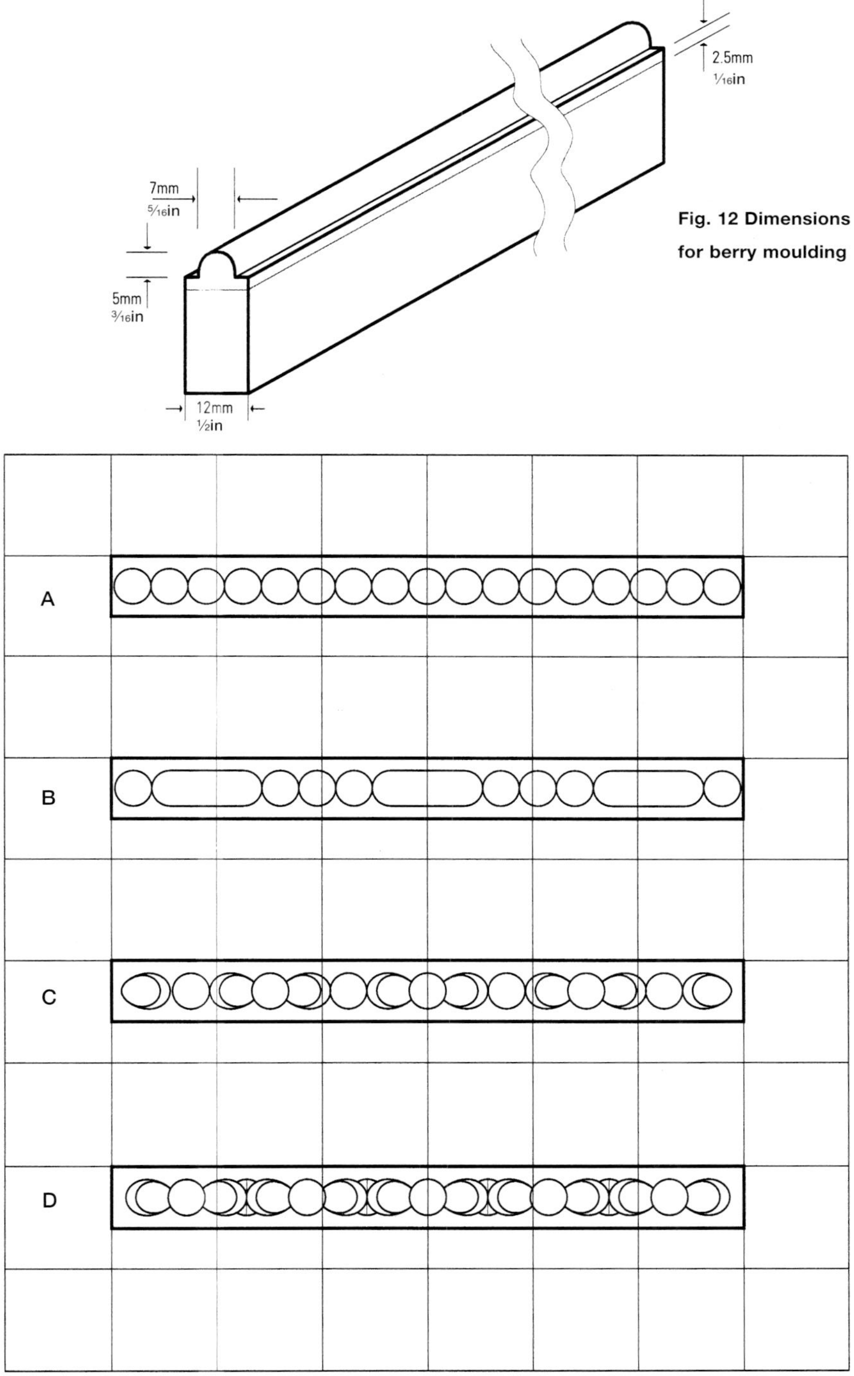

Fig. 12 Dimensions for berry moulding

Fig. 13a Berry moulding; b–d design variations.

(Scale: one square = 20mm (25⁄32in))

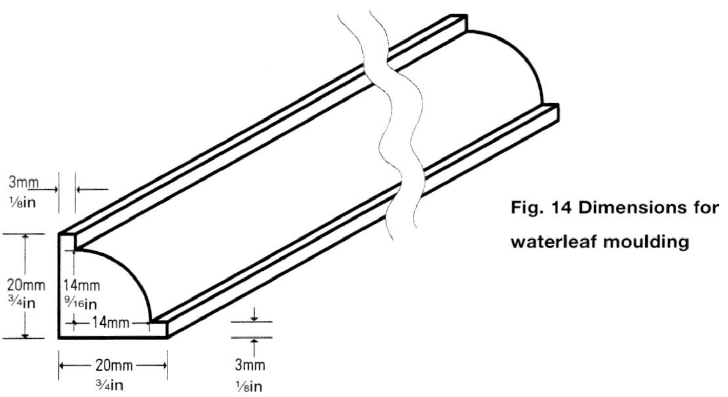

Fig. 14 Dimensions for waterleaf moulding

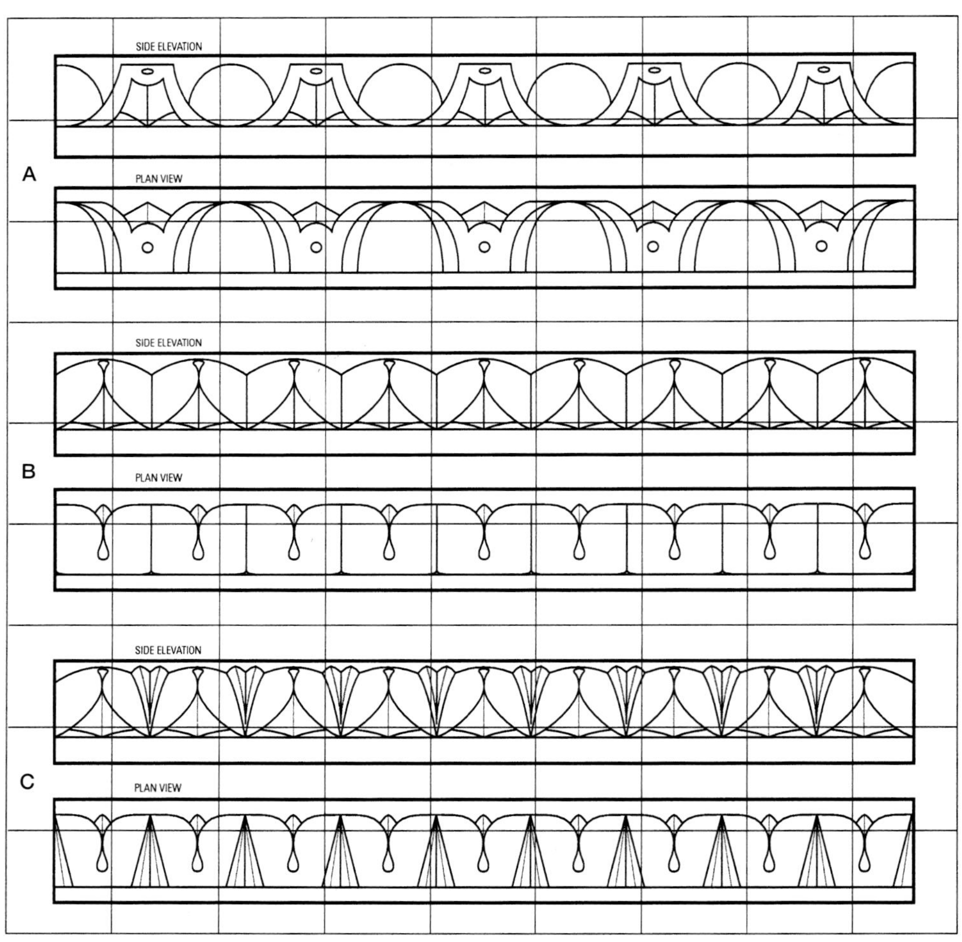

Fig. 15a Egg and dart moulding
b simple waterleaf moulding
c waterleaf moulding

(Scale: one square = 20mm (25⁄32in))

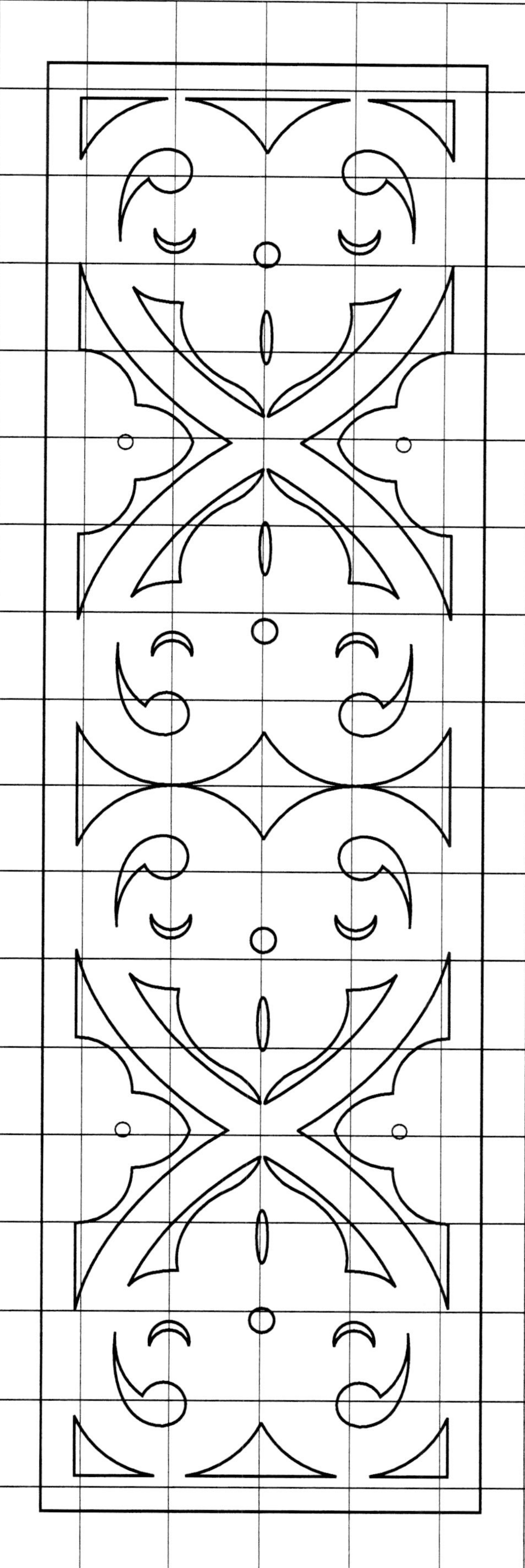

Fig. 16 Flat carving. (Scale: one square = 20mm ($^{25}/_{32}$in))

Fig. 17 Guilloche. (Scale: one square = 20mm ($^{25}/_{32}$in))

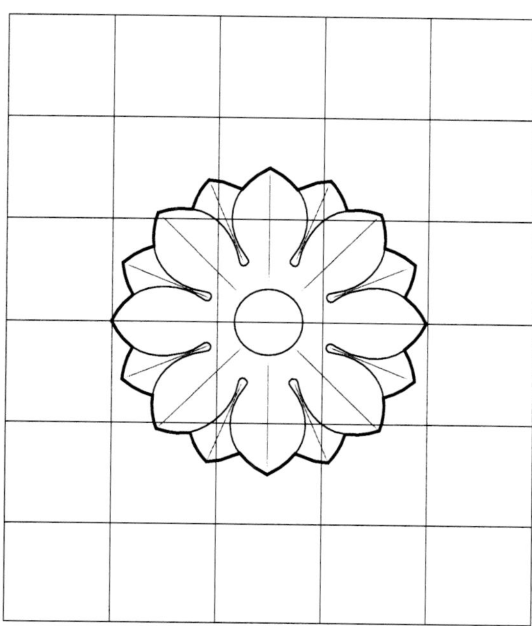

Fig. 18 Patera. (Scale: one square = 20mm (25/32in))

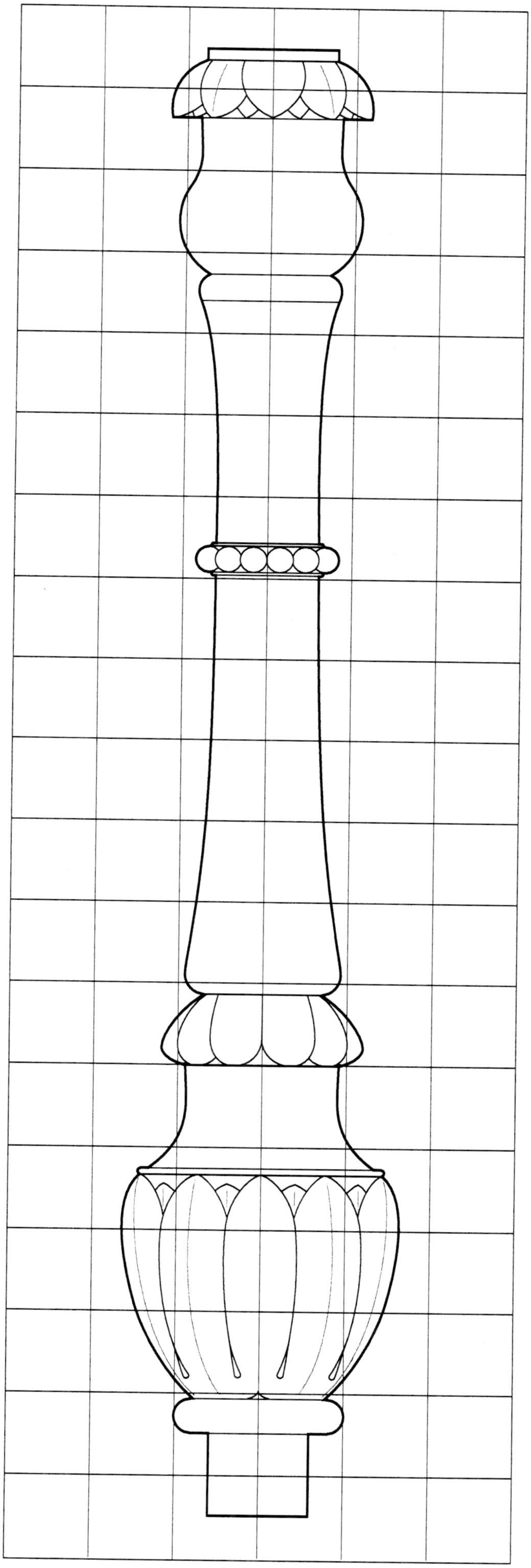

Fig. 19 Candlestick. (Scale: one square = 20mm (25/32in))

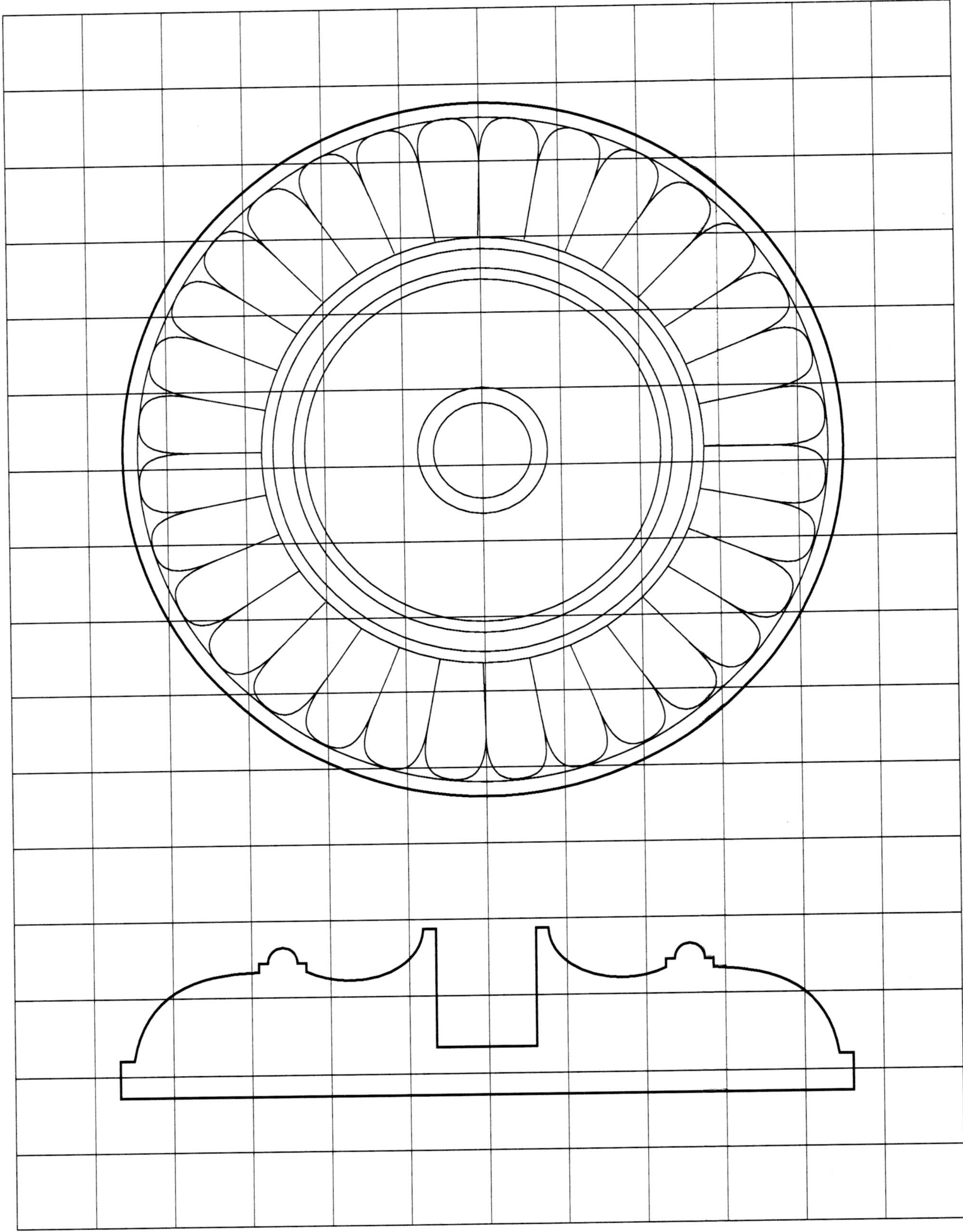

Fig. 20 Candlestick base. (Scale: one square = 20mm (25/32in))

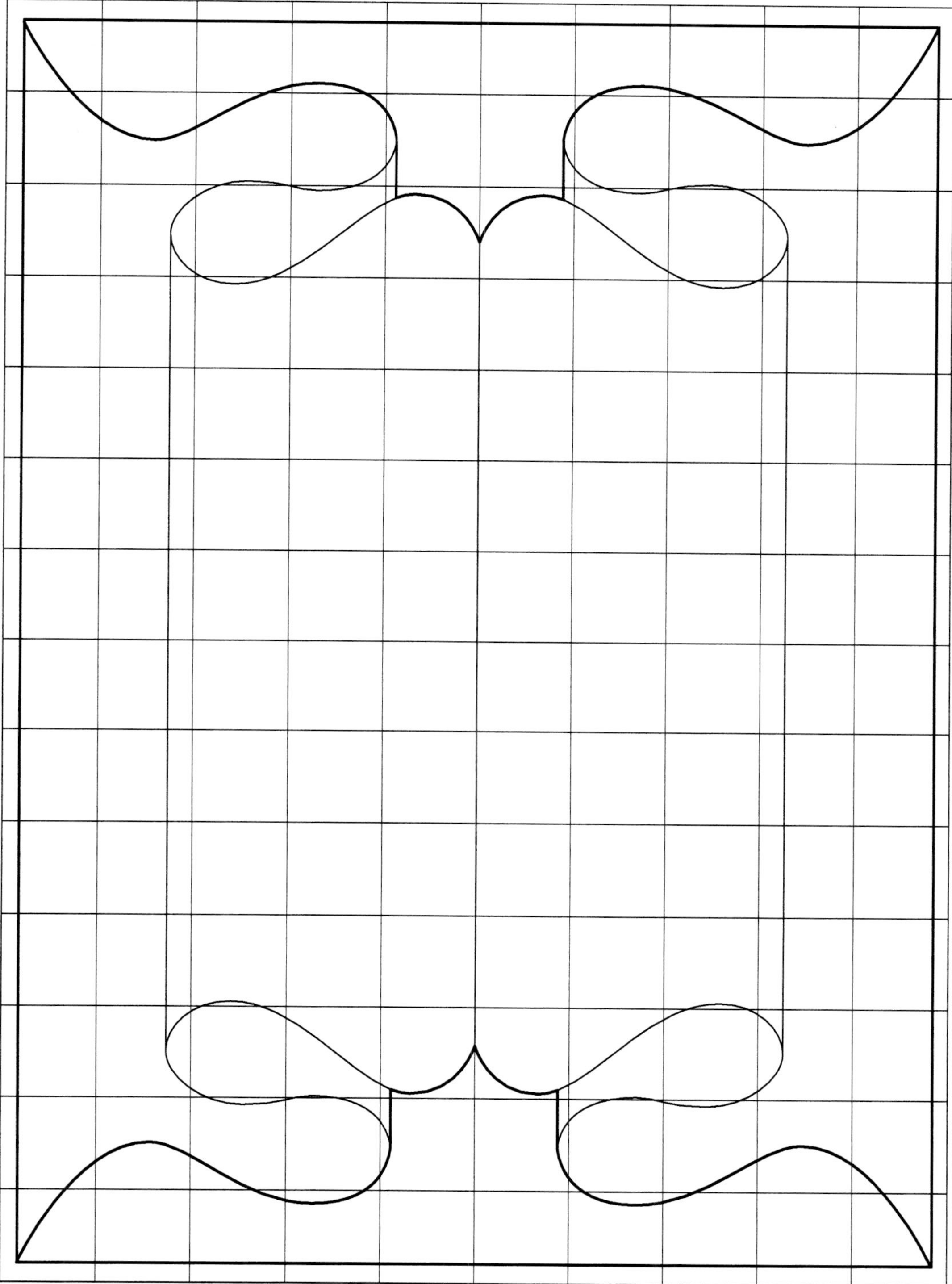

Fig. 21 Linenfold panel. (Scale: one square = 20mm (25⁄32in))

Fig. 22 Tudor rose. (Scale: one square = 20mm (25⁄32in))

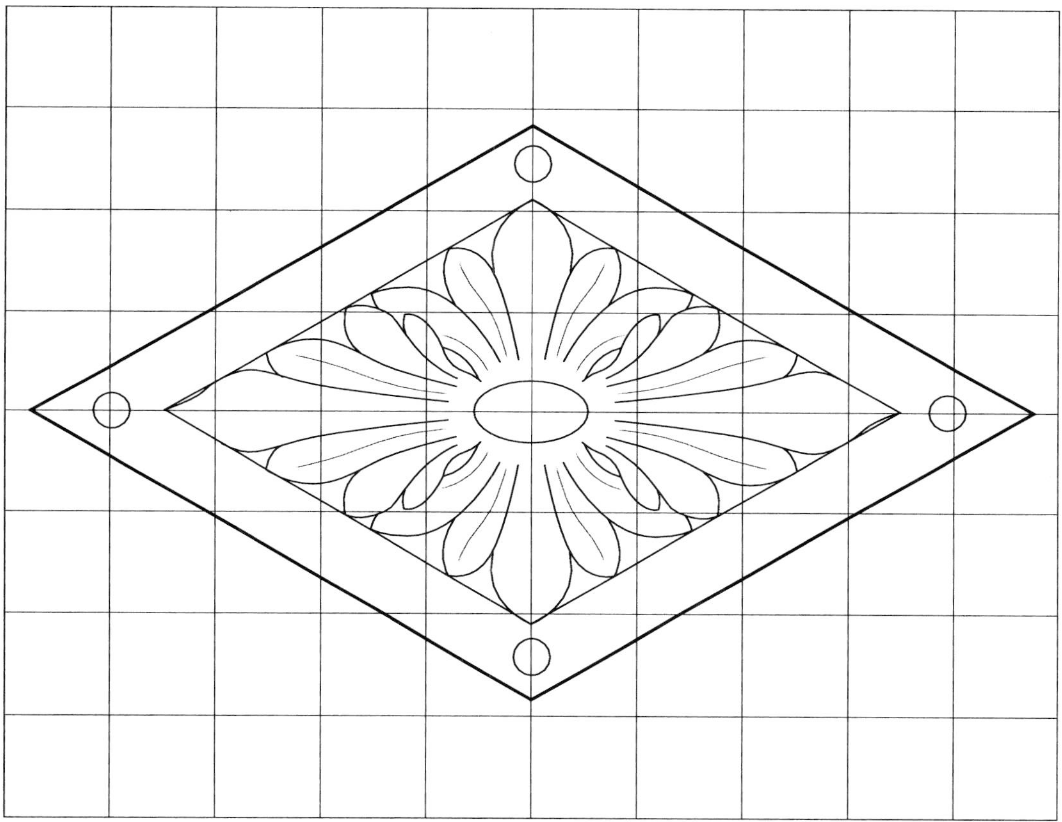

Fig. 23 Acanthus panel. (Scale: one square = 20mm (25⁄32in))

Fig. 24 Old English lettering

Fig. 25 Lettering styles

Fig. 26 Lettering styles

Fig. 27 Flowers and leaves. (Scale: one square = 20mm (25⁄32in))

Fig. 28 Swag. (Scale: one square = 20mm (25⁄32in))

Fig. 29a Corbel front; b corbel side.

(Scale: one square = 20mm (25⁄32in))

Fig. 30a Decorative bracket front.
(Scale: one square = 20mm (25⁄32in)

Fig. 30b Decorative bracket side. (Scale: one square = 20mm ($^{25}/_{32}$in)

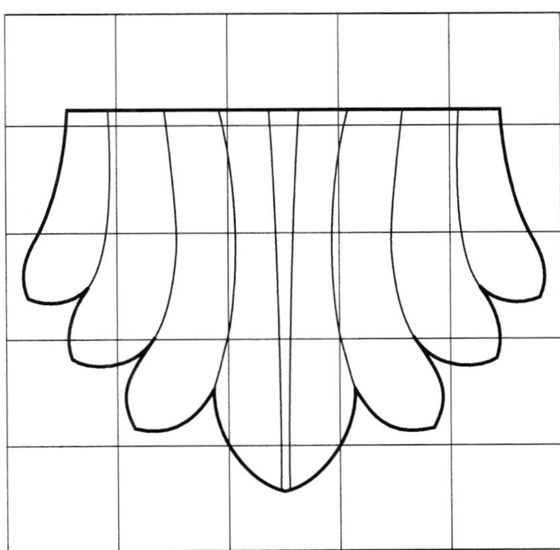

Fig. 30c Decorative bracket end. (Scale: one square = 20mm ($^{25}/_{32}$in)

Design Ideas

If you have enjoyed working through the projects in this book, this section provides an additional set of designs to inspire you to continue to carve. Some, such as the guilloche, are alternative styles of projects featured earlier in the book. For these you will find it helpful to refer to the step-by-step instructions for the original design. Others, such as the decorative pineapple, offer something completely new and for some of these a photograph of the finished carving is provided to show exactly what you need to achieve. In each case, simply photocopy or redraw the illustration to the correct scale (bearing in mind that one square represents 20mm (25⁄32in)), trace it on to your piece of wood and you are ready to start.

Fig. 31a–c Flat carvings

B

C

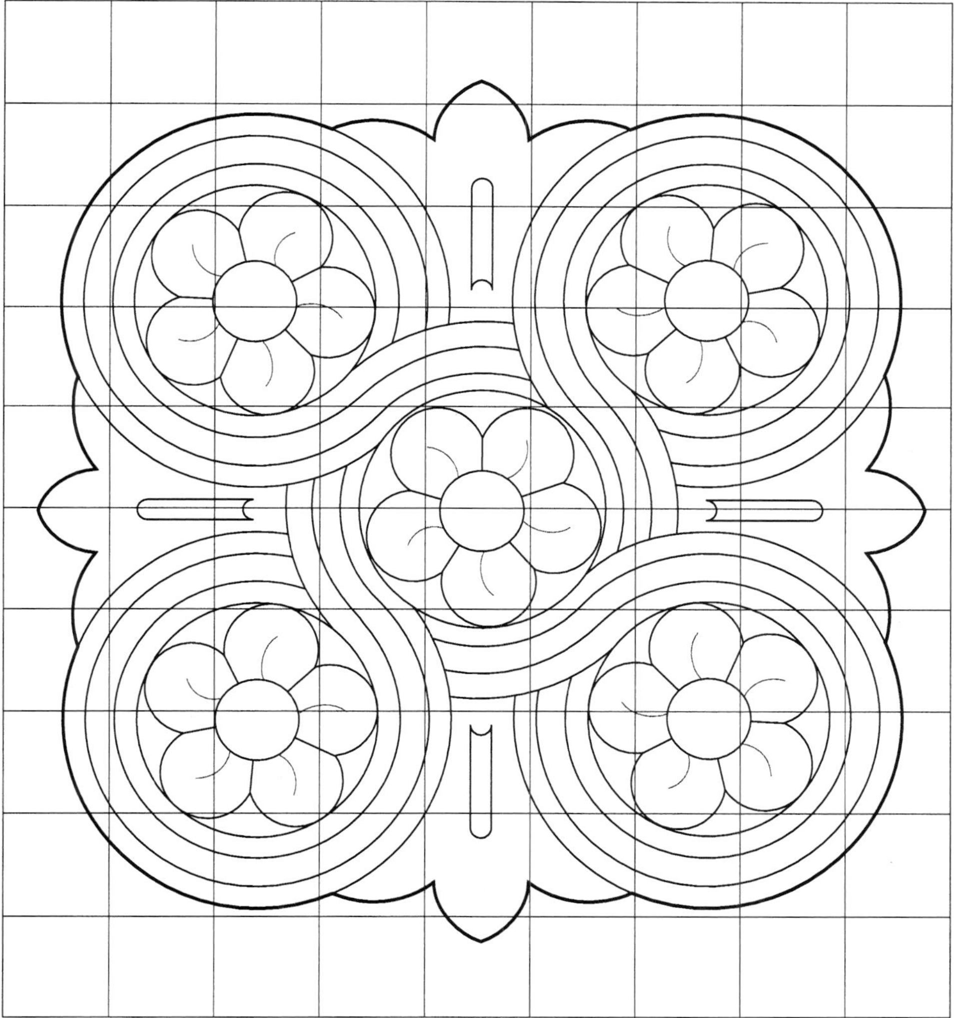

Fig. 32 Guilloche

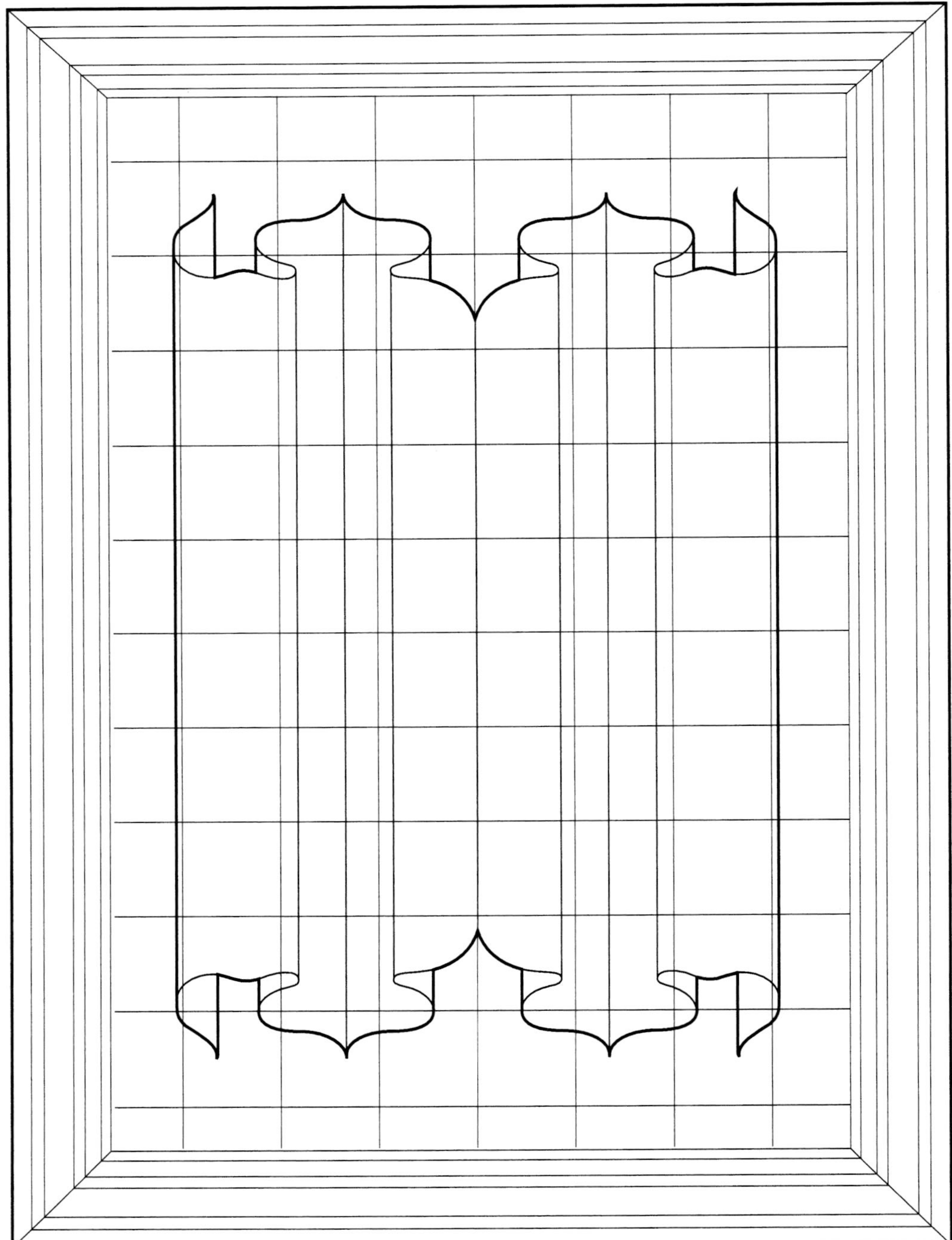

Fig. 33 Linenfold panel

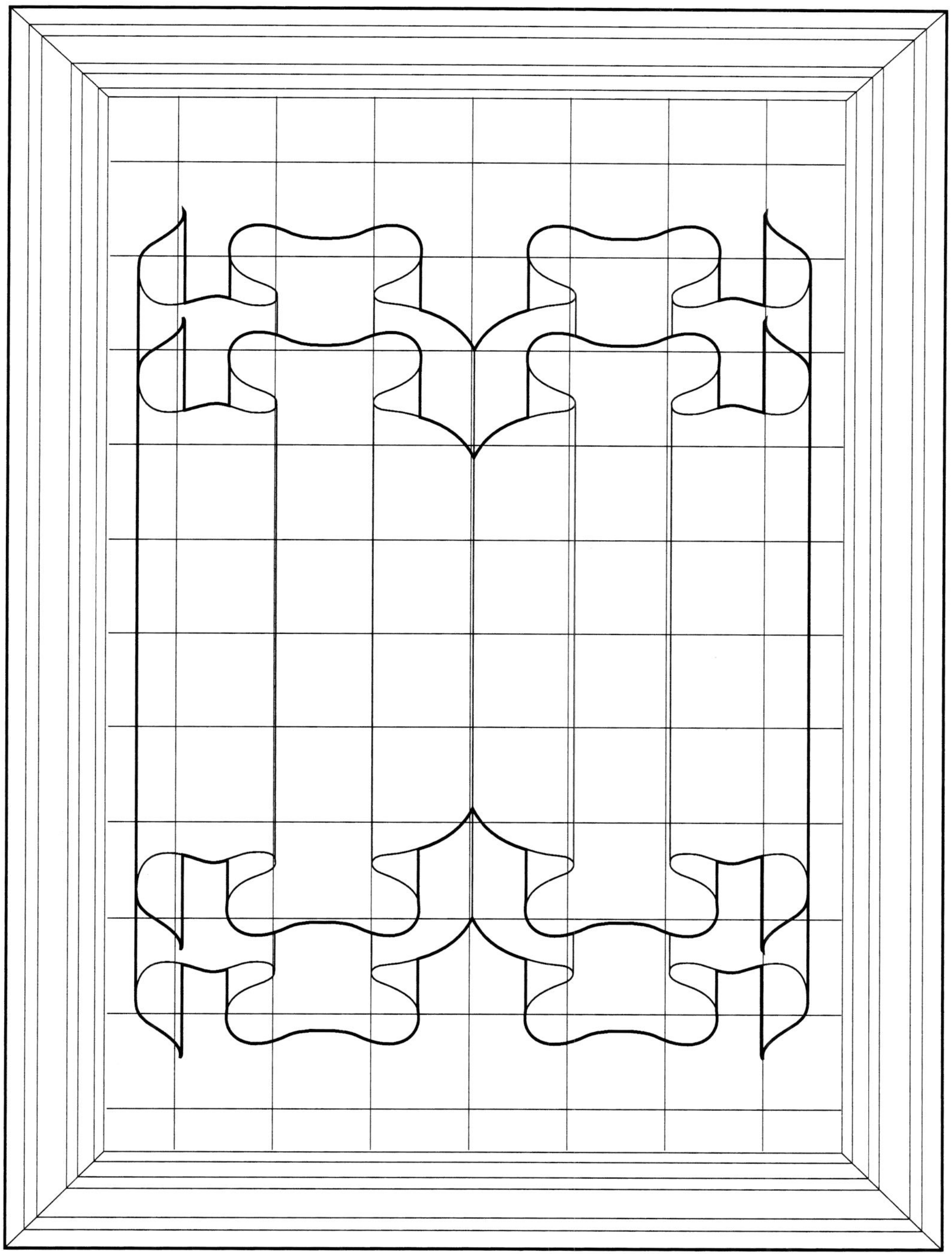

Fig. 34 Linenfold panel

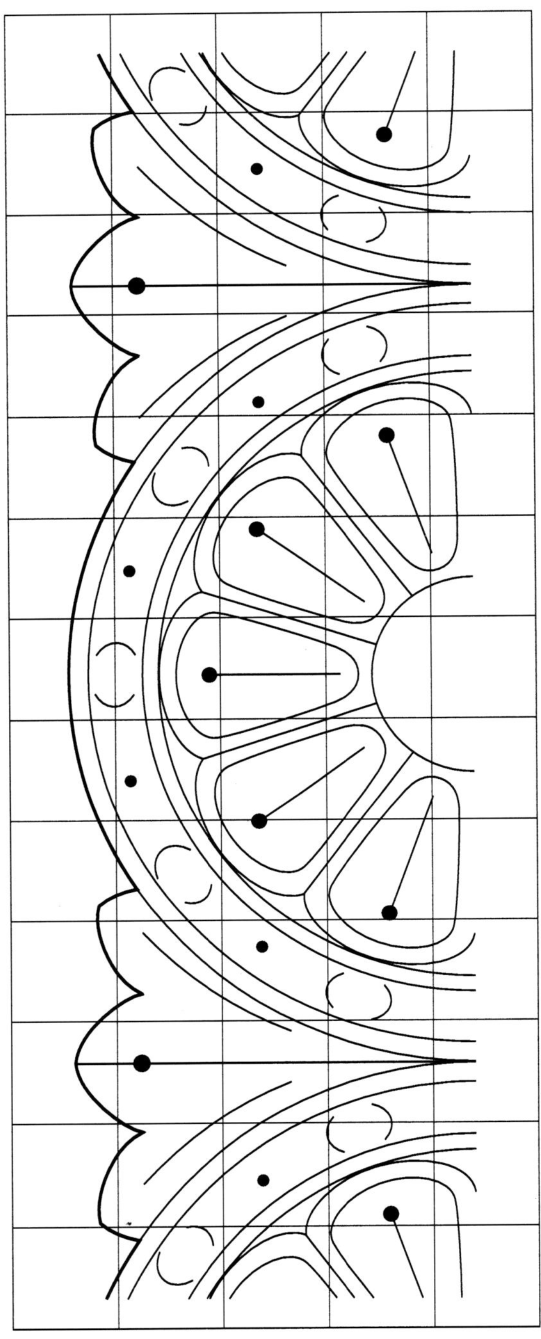

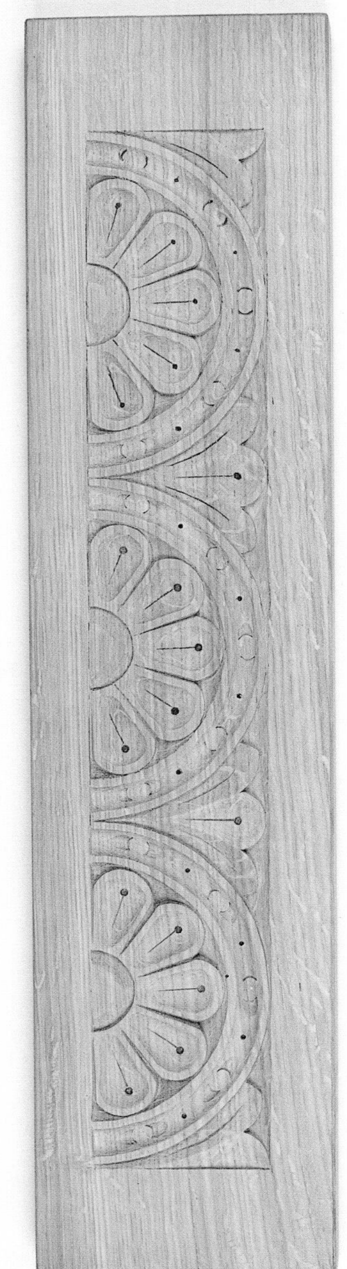

Fig. 35 Lunette

Fig. 36 Lunette

Fig. 38a and b Decorative surround

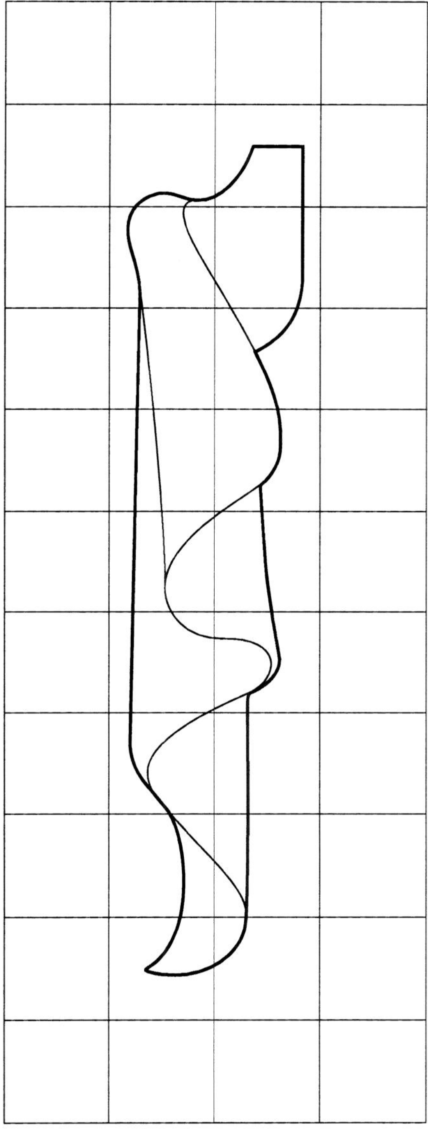

Fig. 38b

Fig. 39a, b and c Decorative pineapple

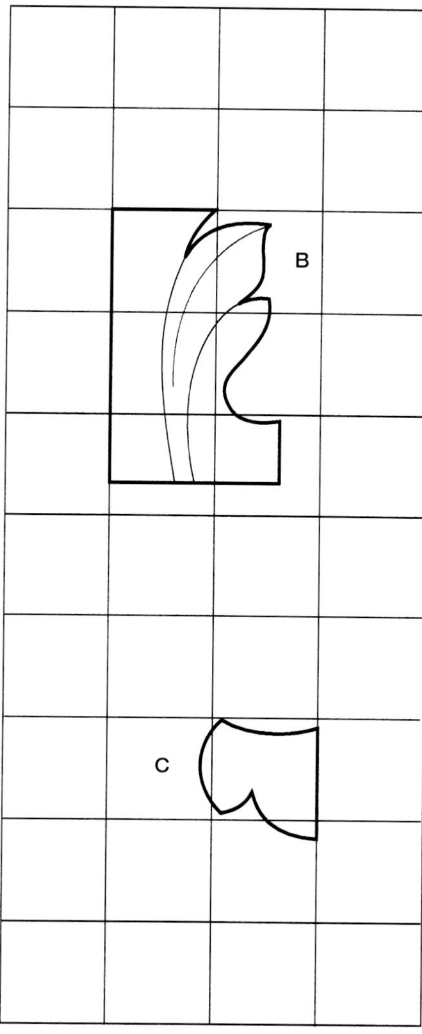

Fig. 39b and c

Fig. 40 Adam-style urn

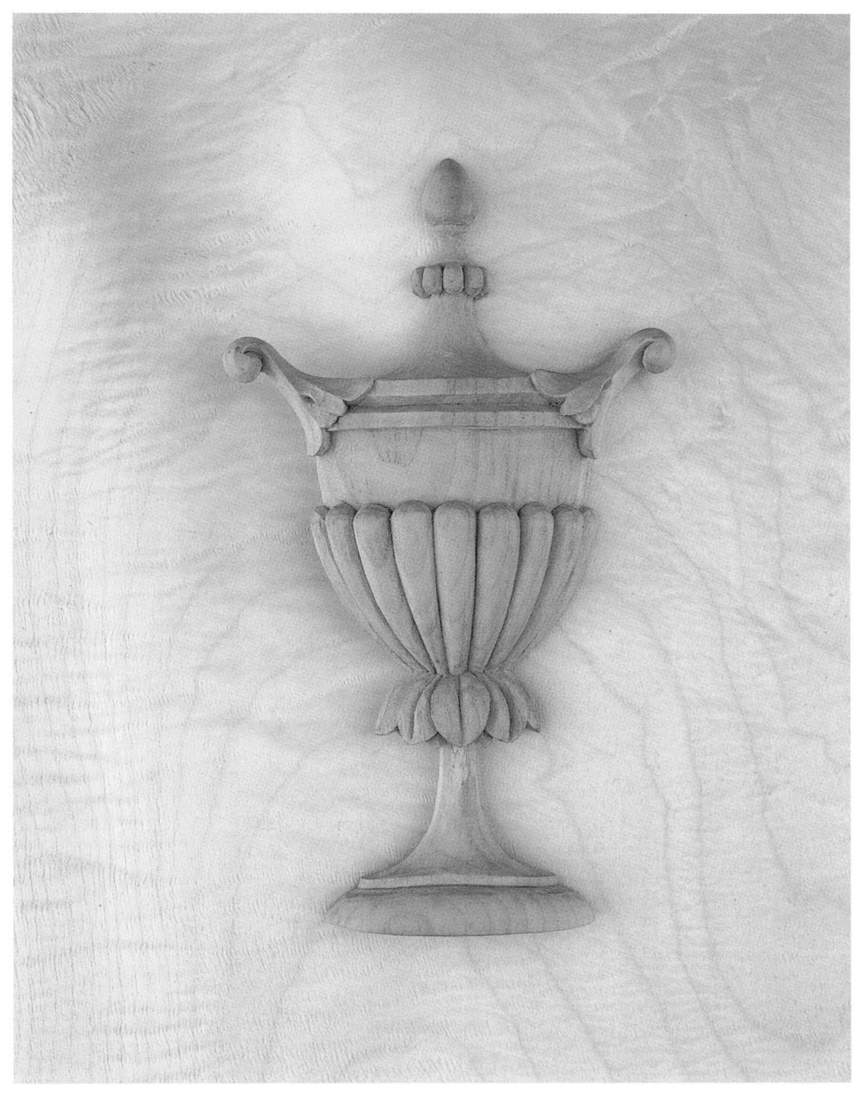

FURTHER INFORMATION

Historical Chart

FRANCE

Dates	Style
121BC–AD500s	Roman
1000–c 1150	Romanesque
c 1150–1500s	Gothic
1515–47	Early Renaissance
1515–1643	Renaissance
1547–89	Mannerist (Henri II)
c 1550–1610	High Renaissance
1589–1610	Henri IV
1610–43	Late Renaissance (Louis XIII)
1643–50	Transition
1643–1715	Baroque (Louis XIV)
1660–1770	Chinoiserie
c 1700–c 25	Régence
1730s–60s	Rococo (Louis XV)
c 1774–90s	Neoclassical (Louis XVI)
1794–1799	Directoire (Style Republicaine)
1799–1804	Consulate
1804–15	Empire (First)
1802–c 15	Egyptiennerie
1814–30	Restoration
1830–48	Rococo Revival (Louis XV)/Louis Philippe
1852–70	Louis XVI Revival/Second Empire
1890s–1910	Art Nouveau (Style Metro)
c 1923–35	Art Deco (Art Moderne)
1930s–	International

Influential Makers and Designers	Dates
Bérain, Jean I	1638–1711
Boulle, André-Charles	1642–1732
Le Brun, Charles	1619–90
Cressent, Charles	1685–1768
Dubois, Jacques	1693–1763
Du Cerceau, Jacques Androuet	c 1520–84
Dunand, Jean	1877–1942
Gallé, Emile	1846–1904
Jacob, Georges	1735–1814
Le Corbusier, Charles	1887–1965
Meissonnier, Juste-Aurèle	1693–1750
Oeben, Jean-François	1721–1763
Riesener, Jean-Henri	1734–1806
Ruhlmann, Jacques-Emile	1879–1933

ITALY

Dates	Style
c 750–c100BC	Etruscan
c 300BC–c 450AD	Roman
530s–1200s	Byzantine
c 800–1400	Romanesque
c 1100–1400	Gothic
1400–1500	Quattrocento Renaissance
1500–1600	Cinquencento Renaissance
c 1560–1700	Baroque
1700–50s	Settocento Rococo
1760s–1840	Neoclassical
1800–50	Italian Directoire
1820–c 1900	Italian Empire
1909–15	Futurist
1922–43	Fascist
1940s–	International
1970s	Post Modern

Influential Makers and Designers	Dates
Bellini, Mario	1935–
Bergamo, Fra Damiano da	c 1490–1550
Colombo, Joe Cesare	1930–71
Galletti, Giovanni	18th century
Juvarra, Filippo	1678–1736
Palladio, Andrea	1518–80
Pantumo, J. di	1492–1556
Piffetti, A. Pietro	1700–77
Piretti, Giancarlo	1940–
Ponti, Gio	a 1960s and 70s
Tosi, Francesco Marie	d 1859
Vitruvius Pollio	1st century BC

BRITAIN

Dates	Style
43–c 410	Roman
1066–c 1150	Romanesque
c 1200–1550s	Gothic
1485–1558	Tudor
1509–1660	Early Renaissance
1558–1603	Elizabethan
1603–49	Early Jacobean
1625–49	Charles I
1649–59	Mid-Jacobean (Cromwellian)
1660–88	Restoration
1675–1770	Chinoiserie
1688–1702	William & Mary
1702–20s	Queen Anne
1714–1830	Georgian
1740s–70s	Chippendale (Rococo)
1760s–90s	Adam (Neoclassical)
1788–90s	Hepplewhite
1791–1806	Sheraton
1795–1837	Regency
1820s–30s	Regency Gothic
1830s–60s	Early Victorian
1836–60s	Elizabethan Revival
1850s–80s	Mid- or High-Victorian
1860s–	Renaissance Revival
1860s–70s	Art Furniture Movement
c 1875–1910	Arts and Crafts Movement
1888–1912	Glasgow School
1890s–1920s	Art Nouveau
c 1920–35	Art Deco
1930s–	International
1942–52	British Utility
1950s	Contemporary
1960s	High Tech

Influential Makers and Designers	Dates
Adam, Robert	1728–1792
Chippendale, Thomas	1718–1779
Eastlake, Charles Lock	1836–1906
Gibbons, Grinling	1648–1720
Gillow, Robert	1703–72
Godwin, Edward William	1833–86
Heal, Sir Ambrose	1872–1959
Hepplewhite, George	1727–1788
Jones, Inigo	1578–1652
Kauffmann, Angelica	1741–1806
Mackintosh, Charles Rennie	1868–1928
Moore, James	c 1670–1726
Morris, William	1834–1896
Pugin, Augustus	1812–1852
Race, Ernest	1913–63
Russell, Sir Gordon	1892–1980
Sheraton, Thomas	1751–1806
Webb, Philip Speakman	1831–1915
Wren, Sir Christopher	1632–1723

USA

Dates	Style
1607–1725	Early Colonial
1614–1664	Dutch Colonial (Baroque)
1700–1725	William & Mary
1720–1755	Queen Anne
1725–90	Late Colonial
1755–1790	Chippendale
c 1780–1810	Early Federal
c 1790–1830	Federal (Neoclassical)
1810–20s	Later Federal
c 1810–30s	Empire
c 1820–50	Gothic Revival
1830s–40s	Restoration/Pillar and Scroll
1830s–40s	Early Victorian
1850s–60s	Louis XVI Revival/Second Empire
1850s–70s	Mid-Victorian
1850s–80s	Renaissance Revival
1860s–70s	Neo Grec
1860s–	Shakers
1879–95	Late Victorian (Eastlake)
1895–1930s	Mission
1930s	Moderne
1930s–	International
1945–	Contemporary
1970s–	High Tech

Influential Makers and Designers	Dates
Affleck, Thomas	a 1740–1795
Allison, Michael	a 1800–1845
Bachman, John	1746–1829
Baudouine, Charles A.	a 1845–1900
Belter, John Henry	1804–1863
Cogswell, John	1769–1782
Connelly, Henry	1770–1826
Goddard, John	a c 1740
Gostelowe, Jonathan	1745–1795
Haines, Ephraim	1775–1811
Hitchcock, Lambert	1795–1852
Hunzinger, George	1835–98
Lannuier, Charles-Honoré	1779–1819
McIntire, Samuel	1757–1811
Meeks and Son, Joseph	a 1797–1868
Phyfe, Duncan	1768–1854
Randolph, Benjamin	1760–1790
Rowland, David	1924–
Savery, William	a 1740–1787
Seymour, John	c 1794
Shoemaker, Jonathon	a 1757
Townsend, John	1732–1809
Trotter, Daniel	1747–1800
Tufft, Thomas	a 1780s
Wright, Frank Lloyd	1869–1959

Metric Conversion Chart

To Convert	To	Multiply By
Inches	Centimeters	2.54
Centimeters	Inches	.4
Feet	Centimeters	30.5
Centimeters	Feet	0.03
Yards	Meters	0.9
Meters	Yards	1.1
Sq. Inches	Sq. Centimeters	6.45
Sq. Centimeters	Sq. Inches	0.16
Sq. Feet	Sq. Meters	0.09
Sq. Meters	Sq. Feet	10.8
Sq. Yards	Sq. Meters	.08
Sq. Meters	Sq. Yards	1.2
Pounds	Kilograms	0.45
Kilograms	Pounds	2.2
Ounces	Grams	28.4
Grams	Ounces	0.04

Suppliers

American Book & Plan Source
3545 Stern Ave.
St. Charles, IL 60174
Phone 630-584-3445
Fax 630-584-3418

Albert Constantine & Son
2050 Eastchester Rd.
Bronx, NY 10461
Phone 718-792-1600
Fax 718-792-2110

Bartley Collection
65 Engerman Ave.
Denton, MO 21629
Phone 410-479-4480
Fax 410-479-4514

Bridge City Tool Works
1104 NE 28th Ave.
Portland, OR 97232
Phone 800-253-3332
Fax 503-287-1085

Craft Supplies USA
1287 E. 1120 S.
Provo, UT 84606
Phone 801-373-0917
Fax 801-374-2879

Eagle America
P.O. Box 1099
510 Center St.
Chardon, OH 44024
Phone 216-286-7429
Fax 216-286-7643

Falls Run Woodcarving, Inc.
9395 Falls Rd.
Girard, PA 16417
Phone 800-524-9077
Fax 814-734-2435

Garrett Wade
161 Avenue of the Americas
New York, NY 10013
Phone 212-807-1155
Fax 212-255-8552

Jesada Tools, Inc.
310 Mears Blvd.
Oldsmar, FL 34677
Phone 813-891-6160
Fax 813-891-6259

Lee Valley Fine Woodworking Tools
12 E. River St.
Odensburg, NY 13669
Phone 800-871-8158

McFeely's
P.O. Box 11169
Lynchburg, VA 24506-1169
Phone 804-846-2729
Fax 804-847-7136

Theta Industrial Products
P.O. Box 70
Mound, MN 55364
Phone 800-441-9870
Fax 612-471-8579

The Tool Chest
45 Emerson Plaza East
P.O. Box 317
Emerson, NJ 07630
Phone 201-261-8665
Fax 201-261-3865

Van Dyke Supply Co.
P.O. Box 278
Woonsocket, SD 57385
Phone 800-558-1234

Wildwood Designs, Inc.
142 E. Court St.
Richland Center, WI 53581
Phone 608-647-2777
Fax 608-647-3066

The Winfield Collection
112 E. Ellen St.
Fenton, MI 48430-2197
Phone 810-629-7712

Woodcraft Supply Corp.
P.O. Box 1686
7845 Emerson Ave.
Parkersburg, WV 26102-1686
Phone 800-225-1153
Fax 304-428-8271

Woodworkers' Discount Books
735 Sunrise Circle
Woodland Park, CO 80863
Phone 719-686-0756
Fax 719-686-0757

The Woodworkers' Store
4365 Willow Dr.
Medina, MN 55340
Phone 800-279-4441
Fax 612-478-8395

Woodworker's Supply, Inc.
1108 North Glenn Rd.
Casper, WY 82601
Phone 800-645-9292
Fax 307-821-7331

William Alden Company
27 Stuart St.
Boston, MA 02116
Phone 800-249-8665
Fax 617-426-3430

Woodsmith Store
2625 Beaver Ave.
Des Moines, IA 50310
Phone 515-255-8979
Fax 515-255-8857

Index

Page references in *italic* indicate illustrations; references in **bold** indicate plan drawings.